Incomplete Data and Data Dependencies in Relational Databases

Synthesis Lectures on Data Management

Editor
M. Tamer Özsu, *University of Waterloo*

Synthesis Lectures on Data Management is edited by Tamer Özsu of the University of Waterloo. The series will publish 50- to 125 page publications on topics pertaining to data management. The scope will largely follow the purview of premier information and computer science conferences, such as ACM SIGMOD, VLDB, ICDE, PODS, ICDT, and ACM KDD. Potential topics include, but not are limited to: query languages, database system architectures, transaction management, data warehousing, XML and databases, data stream systems, wide scale data distribution, multimedia data management, data mining, and related subjects.

Declarative Networking
Boon Thau Loo and Wenchao Zhou
2012

Full-Text (Substring) Indexes in External Memory
Marina Barsky, Ulrike Stege, and Alex Thomo
2011

Spatial Data Management
Nikos Mamoulis
2011

Database Repairing and Consistent Query Answering
Leopoldo Bertossi
2011

Managing Event Information: Modeling, Retrieval, and Applications
Amarnath Gupta and Ramesh Jain
2011

Fundamentals of Physical Design and Query Compilation
David Toman and Grant Weddell
2011

Methods for Mining and Summarizing Text Conversations
Giuseppe Carenini, Gabriel Murray, and Raymond Ng
2011

Probabilistic Databases
Dan Suciu, Dan Olteanu, Christopher Ré, and Christoph Koch
2011

Peer-to-Peer Data Management
Karl Aberer
2011

Probabilistic Ranking Techniques in Relational Databases
Ihab F. Ilyas and Mohamed A. Soliman
2011

Uncertain Schema Matching
Avigdor Gal
2011

Fundamentals of Object Databases: Object-Oriented and Object-Relational Design
Suzanne W. Dietrich and Susan D. Urban
2010

Incomplete Data and Data Dependencies in Relational Databases
Sergio Greco, Cristian Molinaro, and Francesca Spezzano

ISBN: 978-3-031-00765-1   paperback
ISBN: 978-3-031-01893-0   ebook

DOI 10.1007/978-3-031-01893-0

A Publication in the Springer series
SYNTHESIS LECTURES ON DATA MANAGEMENT

Lecture #29
Series Editor: M. Tamer Özsu, *University of Waterloo*
Series ISSN
Synthesis Lectures on Data Management
Print 2153-5418   Electronic 2153-5426

Incomplete Data
and Data Dependencies
in Relational Databases

Sergio Greco, Cristian Molinaro, and Francesca Spezzano
DEIS, Università della Calabria

SYNTHESIS LECTURES ON DATA MANAGEMENT #29

ABSTRACT

The *chase* has long been used as a central tool to analyze dependencies and their effect on queries. It has been applied to different relevant problems in database theory such as query optimization, query containment and equivalence, dependency implication, and database schema design. Recent years have seen a renewed interest in the chase as an important tool in several database applications, such as data exchange and integration, query answering in incomplete data, and many others.

It is well known that the chase algorithm might be non-terminating and thus, in order for it to find practical applicability, it is crucial to identify cases where its termination is guaranteed. Another important aspect to consider when dealing with the chase is that it can introduce *null* values into the database, thereby leading to incomplete data. Thus, in several scenarios where the chase is used the problem of dealing with data dependencies and incomplete data arises.

This book discusses fundamental issues concerning data dependencies and incomplete data with a particular focus on the chase and its applications in different database areas. We report recent results about the crucial issue of identifying conditions that guarantee the chase termination. Different database applications where the chase is a central tool are discussed with particular attention devoted to query answering in the presence of data dependencies and database schema design.

KEYWORDS

incomplete databases, inconsistent databases, data dependencies, chase algorithm, consistent query answers

Contents

Acknowledgments

The authors are indebted to many researchers who have worked for several years on the topics of this book. Their excellent papers have been an important source, which has made possible to write this monograph. Of course, we are the only responsible for possible errors.

We thank Leo Bertossi for his valuable and detailed comments. The book greatly benefited from his suggestions. We would like to thank Tamer Özsu for inviting us to write this book and for his suggestions on the preliminary draft.

Finally, we would like to thank Diane Cerra for her constant help.

Sergio Greco, Cristian Molinaro, and Francesca Spezzano
July 2012

CHAPTER 1

Introduction

The study of data dependencies started with the beginning of the relational data model itself and attracted a great deal of interest throughout the 1970s and early 1980s [Armstrong, 1974, Codd, 1972, Fagin and Vardi, 1986, Vardi]. Data dependencies have long been used to express *integrity constraints* on data, that is semantic properties that database instances should satisfy to properly reflect the real state of the world. Furthermore, data dependencies have been used in database schema design to define *normal forms*, i.e., conditions that a "good" relational database schema has to satisfy in order to reduce or eliminate redundant information [Bernstein, 1976, Fagin, 1977b]. In this context, the *chase* (first introduced in [Maier et al., 1979]) has been a central tool to analyze dependencies and their effect on queries. Besides being applied for dependency implication and database schema design, it has been applied to other relevant problems in database theory such as query optimization, query containment, and equivalence [Kolaitis and Vardi, 2000].

Recent years have seen a renewed interest in data dependencies and, as an immediate consequence, in the chase. In fact, data dependencies play a central role in several current database applications such as data exchange and integration [Fagin et al., 2005a, Lenzerini, 2002] and ontology management [Cali et al., 2009a,b]. In data integration dependencies are used to describe data in a global schema in terms of data in local schemas, whereas in data exchange they are used to describe data in a target schema in terms of data in a source schema, and actually produce the target database.

It is well known that the chase algorithm might be non-terminating and thus, in order for it to find practical applicability, it is crucial to identify cases where its termination is guaranteed [Greco et al., 2011]. Another important aspect to consider when dealing with the chase is that it can introduce *null* values into the database thereby leading to incomplete data. Thus, in several scenarios where the chase is used the problem of dealing with data dependencies and incomplete data arises.

This book discusses fundamental issues concerning data dependencies and incomplete data with a particular focus on the chase and its applications in different database areas. We report recent results about the crucial issue of identifying conditions that guarantee the chase termination. Different database applications where the chase is a central tool are discussed, with particular attention devoted to query answering in the presence of data dependencies [ten Cate et al., 2012] and database schema design [Darwen et al., 2012].

In the context of database design, checking the implication of certain dependencies is an important issue, in order to verify whether a database schema complies with the conditions imposed by a normal form. This issue can be tackled by leveraging the chase.

In the context of data integration, data exchange, and repairing inconsistent databases, the enforcement of tuple-generating dependencies is done by inserting new tuples into the database. Such a process can be accomplished again by applying chase algorithm, although it might be non-terminating and thus guaranteeing its termination becomes a central issue.

CHAPTER 2

Relational Databases

A database is a collection of data organized to model relevant aspects of reality and support processes requiring this information.

A database model is a theory or specification describing how a database is structured and used. It provides the means for specifying particular data structures, constraining the data sets associated with these structures, and manipulating the data. The most popular example of a database model is the *relational model*, although several other data models have been proposed and are currently used (e.g., hierarchical model, network model, object model). The relational model was introduced by E. F. Codd in 1970 (see [Codd, 1970]) as a way to make Database Management Systems (DBMSs) independent of any particular application. It is a mathematical model defined in terms of predicate logic and set theory.

In this chapter we recall the basic notions of the relational model, relational query languages, and the basic types of data dependencies.

2.1 RELATIONAL MODEL

We assume the existence of the following pairwise disjoint sets: a countably infinite set $Consts$ of *constants*, a countably infinite set $\mathcal{A}$ of *attributes*, and a countably infinite set $\mathcal{R}$ of *relation names*; $Consts$ is also called *database domain*. Each attribute $A_i \in \mathcal{A}$ is associated with a set of constants called *attribute domain* and denoted as $dom(A_i)$. Each relation name $R \in \mathcal{R}$ is associated with a finite sequence of attributes $A_1, \ldots, A_n$, where n is the *arity* of R. We say that $R(A_1, \ldots, A_n)$ is a *relation schema*; such a relation schema will also be referred to as $R(U)$, where $U = \{A_1, \ldots, A_n\}$. A *relation* r over $R(A_1, \ldots, A_n)$ is a finite subset of $dom(A_1) \times \cdots \times dom(A_n)$. We also say that r is a relation of R. Each element t of r is called a *tuple*. We use $t[A_i]$ to denote the A_i-component of t. Likewise, for a set of attributes $X \subseteq \{A_1, \ldots, A_n\}$, $t[X]$ denotes the restriction of t to X. A *database schema* is a non-empty finite set $\mathbf{R} = \{R_1(U_1), \ldots, R_m(U_m)\}$ of relation schemas. A *database instance* (or simply database) D over $\mathbf{R}$ is a finite set of relations $\{r_1, \ldots, r_m\}$, where each r_i is a relation over $R_i(U_i)$. To denote a tuple t belonging to a relation over schema $R_i(U_i)$, we will use the notation $R_i(t)$ and call $R_i(t)$ a *fact*; hence, a database can be viewed as a finite set of facts.

Functional dependencies, keys, and foreign keys. *Data dependencies* (also called *integrity constraints*) express semantic information about data, i.e., relationships that should hold among data. Below we present some of the most common kinds of data dependencies and will come back to data dependencies in Chapter 6, where a more complete treatment is provided. To give an example, consider a database schema consisting of the following two relation schemas: $Employee(E\#, EName, Dept)$ and $Department(D\#, DName)$. In this case, we may want to impose the condition that every relation over the first relation schema cannot contain two different tuples with the same id (i.e., the same value on $E\#$). Likewise, every relation over the second relation schema cannot contain two different tuples with the same id (i.e., the same value on $D\#$). Furthermore, it would be reasonable to impose the condition that every department code appearing in the employee relation must appear in the department relation too. The first two constraints mentioned above are examples of *key constraints*—we say that attribute $E\#$ is a key of $Employee$ and $D\#$ is a key of $Department$. The last constraint mentioned above is an example of *foreign key constraint*—we say that attribute $Dept$ of $Employee$ is a foreign key (referring to attribute $D\#$ of $Department$). Key and foreign key constraints are special types of *functional* and *inclusion dependencies*.

Example 2.1   Consider the following database.

E#	Ename	Dept
e1	John	d1
e2	Peter	d2
e3	Craig	d3

D#	Dname
d1	Physics
d2	Chemistry

Attribute $E\#$ is a key of the first relation, whereas attribute $D\#$ is a key of the second one (this is illustrated by underlining $E\#$ and $D\#$). The foreign key constraint stating that each department appearing in the employee relation must appear in the department relation can be denoted with the expression $Employee[Dept] \subseteq Department[D\#]$. While the database above satisfies the key constraints, it is easy to see that the foreign key constraint is not satisfied because there is no tuple in the department relation having $d3$ as $D\#$-value.   □

Given a relation schema $R(U)$, a *functional dependency* fd over $R(U)$ is an expression of the form $X \rightarrow Y$, where $X, Y \subseteq U$. If Y is a single attribute, then fd is said to be in *standard form* whereas if $Y \subseteq X$, then the functional dependency is *trivial*. A relation r over $R(U)$ *satisfies* fd, denoted as $r \models fd$, iff $\forall t_1, t_2 \in r$, $t_1[X] = t_2[X]$ implies $t_1[Y] = t_2[Y]$ (we also say that r is *consistent* with respect to fd). Moreover, r satisfies (or is consistent w.r.t.) a set FD of functional dependencies over $R(U)$, denoted as $r \models FD$, iff r satisfies every functional dependency in FD. We say that FD *logically implies* a functional dependency fd, denoted $FD \models fd$, iff for every relation r over $R(U)$, if r satisfies FD, then r satisfies fd. A *key dependency* is a functional dependency of the form $X \rightarrow U$. Given a set FD of functional dependencies, a *key* of R is a minimal (under set inclusion) set K of attributes of R such that FD logically implies $K \rightarrow U$. Each attribute in K is called *key attribute*. A *primary key* of R is a designated key of R. Given two relation schemas $R(U)$ and $S(V)$, a *foreign key constraint* fk is an expression of the form $R(W) \subseteq S(Z)$, where $W \subseteq U, Z \subseteq V, |W| = |Z|$ and Z is a key of S (if Z is the primary key of S we call fk a *primary foreign key constraint*). Two relations r and s over $R(U)$ and $S(V)$, respectively, *satisfy* fk iff for each tuple $t_1 \in r$ there is a tuple $t_2 \in s$ such that $t_1[W] = t_2[Z]$ (we also say that r and s are *consistent* with respect to fk).

2.2   QUERY LANGUAGES

Query languages are introduced to derive information from databases. A *query* Q is a function that takes a database D as input (i.e., a set of relations) and gives a relation as output. The result of applying Q to D is denoted by $Q(D)$. Queries can be expressed by means of a given query language, such as *relational algebra*, *relational calculus* or *SQL* (Structured Query Language). The expressive power of a language is measured in terms of the set of queries that can be expressed using the language.

2.2.1   RELATIONAL ALGEBRA

Relational algebra extends the algebra of sets and consists of five primitive operators. Consider two relation schemas $R(A_1, \ldots, A_n)$ and $S(B_1, \ldots, B_m)$ and let r and s be two relations over the first and second schema, respectively. The primitive relational algebra operators are defined as follows.

- *Cartesian product*: $r \times s = \{(r_1, \ldots, r_n, s_1, \ldots, s_m) \mid (r_1, \ldots, r_n) \in r \wedge (s_1, \ldots, s_m) \in s\}$.

- *Union*: $r \cup s = \{t \mid t \in r \vee t \in s\}$.

- *Difference*: $r - s = \{t \mid t \in r \wedge t \notin s\}$.

- *Projection*: $\pi_A(r) = \{t[A] \mid t \in r\}$, where $A \subseteq \{A_1, \ldots, A_n\}$.

- *Selection*: $\sigma_F(r) = \{t \mid t \in r \wedge F(t)\}$. Here F is a boolean expression built using propositional logical connectives and atomic expressions of the form $E_1 \ op \ E_2$ where op is a comparison operator, whereas E_1 and E_2 are constants or attributes names. $F(t)$ denotes the boolean value given by evaluating expression F over tuple t.

The relational algebra defined above is also called *named*, since attribute names are used in the relational algebra operators—in the *unnamed* relational algebra attributes are referred to by their positions in the relation schema. In the named relational algebra we also have a unary operator called *renaming* defined as follows: $\rho_{A_1/B_1, \ldots, A_k/B_k}(r)$, where the A_i's and B_j's are attribute names such that $A_i \neq B_i$, returns the input relation r with a schema derived from the schema of r by renaming each attribute A_i as B_i, for $i = 1, \ldots, k$.

Several derived operators have been defined as well. Derived operators do not increase the expressive power of the language (i.e., they do not allow us to express further queries), but are introduced to make expressions more comprehensible and their evaluation more efficient. For instance, the derived operators intersection and (theta) join are defined as follows.

- *Intersection*: $r \cap s = \{t \mid t \in r \wedge t \in s\} = r - (r - s) = s - (s - r)$.

- *Join*: $r \bowtie_F s = \{(r_1, \ldots, r_n, s_1, \ldots, s_m) \mid (r_1, \ldots, r_n) \in r \wedge (s_1, \ldots, s_m) \in s \wedge F(r_1, \ldots, r_n, s_1, \ldots, s_m)\} = \sigma_F(r \times s)$, where F is a selection expression.

There exist several other derived operators such as natural join, different types of outer joins and semi-join, division, etc.

Example 2.2 Suppose to have two relations, *employee* and *department*, over schema *Employee*(*E#, EName, Dept*) and *Department*(*D#, DName*), respectively. The query asking for the names of the employees who work in the department *Physics* can be expressed as:

$$\pi_{Ename}\left(employee \bowtie_{Dept=D\#} \sigma_{Dname=\text{``}Physics\text{''}}(department)\right). \qquad \square$$

The set of queries expressible in relational algebra will be denoted by $\mathcal{RA}$.

2.2.2 RELATIONAL CALCULUS

Another formalism to express queries in the relational model is *relational calculus*, described below. More precisely, the language we present in this subsection is sometimes called *domain calculus*, because variables range over the underlying database domain; in *tuple calculus*, that we do not consider, variables range over tuples.

The existence of a set V of variables is assumed. Recall that $Consts$ is used to denote the database domain. A *term* is a constant in $Consts$ or a variable in V. *Formulas* are inductively defined as follows:

- a (basic) formula, also called *atom*, is: (i) an expression of the form $R(w_1, \ldots, w_n)$ where R is a relation name with arity n and the w_i's are terms—this is called a *standard atom*; or (ii) an expression of the form $w_1 \; op \; w_2$ where w_1, w_2 are terms and op is a comparison operator (i.e., $op \in \{>, <, \geq, \leq, =, \neq\}$)—this is called a *built-in atom*.

- if G and H are formulas, then $(G \wedge H)$, $(G \vee H)$, $\neg G$ are formulas;

- if x is a variable in V and G is a formula, then $\exists x G$ and $\forall x G$ are formulas.

We now define *free* variable occurrences. An occurrence of a variable x in a formula F is said to be *free* if one of the following holds:

- F is a basic formula;

- $F = \neg G$ and the occurrence of x is free in G;

- $F = G \wedge H$ (resp. $F = G \vee H$) and the occurrence of x is free in G or H;

- $F = \exists y.G$ (resp. $F = \forall y.G$), x and y are distinct variables, and the occurrence of x is free in G.

We use $free(F)$ to denote the set of free variables of F, i.e., the variables appearing in F having at least one free occurrence in F.

A *relational calculus query* is an expression of the form:

$$\{(u_1, \ldots, u_n) \mid F\},$$

where the u_i's are terms (the same term can be repeated), F is a formula, and the variables in $\{u_1, \ldots, u_n\}$ are exactly the free variables of F.

Example 2.3 Consider again the database schema consisting of the two relation schemas $Employee(E\#, EName, Dept)$ and $Department(D\#, DName)$. The query asking for the names of the employees working in the $Physics$ department is expressed by the following relational calculus query:

$$\{(y) \mid \exists x\, \exists z\, Employee(x, y, z) \wedge Department(z, Physics)\}. \qquad \square$$

The semantics of a relational calculus query over a database is defined with respect to a particular domain $Consts'$, called *evaluation domain*, which is intended to specify the constants over which variables can range. Before defining the semantics of relational calculus queries, we introduce some notations and terminology used in the following. A *valuation* for a set of variables $V' \subseteq V$ is a mapping $\dot{\nu}: V' \cup Consts \rightarrow Consts$ such that $\nu(c) = c$ for every $c \in Consts$. We use $\nu|_{V''}$ to denote the restriction of ν to $V'' \subseteq V'$. The *active domain* of a database D, denoted $adom(D)$, is the set of constants appearing in D. Likewise, we use $adom(Q)$ and $adom(F)$ to denote the set of constants appearing in relational calculus query Q and formula F, respectively.

Let D be a database, $Consts'$ be the *evaluation domain* such that $adom(D) \subseteq Consts' \subseteq Consts$, F a formula such that $adom(F) \subseteq Consts'$, and ν a valuation for the free variables of F with range contained in $Consts'$. Then, we say that D *satisfies* F for ν *relative* to $Consts'$, denoted $D \models F[\nu]$ ($Consts'$ is understood), if one of the following holds.

- $F = R(w_1, \ldots, w_m)$ and $R(\nu(w_1), \ldots, \nu(w_m))$ is a fact of D.

- $F = w_1 \; op \; w_2$, with $op \in \{>, <, \geq, \leq, =, \neq\}$, and $\nu(w_1) \; op \; \nu(w_2)$ is true.

- $F = G \wedge H$, $D \models G[\nu|_{free(G)}]$, and $D \models H[\nu|_{free(H)}]$.

- $F = G \vee H$. In addition, $D \models G[\nu|_{free(G)}]$ or $D \models H[\nu|_{free(H)}]$.

- $F = \neg G$ and $D \models G[\nu|_{free(G)}]$ does not hold.

- $F = \exists x.G$ and for some $c \in Consts'$, $D \models G[\nu']$, where ν' is a valuation for x and the variables of ν such that $\nu'(x) = c$ and $\nu'(y) = \nu(y)$ for any other variable y.

- $F = \forall x.G$ and for every $c \in Consts'$, $D \models G[v']$, where v' is a valuation for x and the variables of v such that $v'(x) = c$ and $v'(y) = v(y)$ for any other variable y.

We define the semantics of a relational calculus query $Q = \{(u_1, \ldots, u_n) \mid F\}$ over a database D with respect to the evaluation domain $Consts'$, where $(adom(D) \cup adom(Q)) \subseteq Consts' \subseteq Consts$. The role of $Consts'$ is to specify the constants over which variables can range. Notice that the supersets of $adom(D) \cup adom(Q)$ are the only domains with respect to which it makes sense to evaluate Q over D. We define the semantics of Q over D with respect to $Consts'$ as follows:

$$Q_{Consts'}(D) = \{ \quad (v(u_1), \ldots, v(u_n)) \mid$$
$$D \models F[v] \text{ and } v \text{ is a valuation for } free(F) \text{ with range } \subseteq Consts' \} .$$

When $Consts' = Consts$ the semantics above corresponds to the standard interpretation of predicate calculus. Note that if $Consts'$ is infinite, then $Q_{Consts'}(D)$ can be an infinite set of tuples. The set of queries that can be expressed with relational calculus will be denoted as $\mathcal{RC}$.

2.2.3   DOMAIN INDEPENDENT AND SAFE RC QUERIES

A relational calculus query Q is *domain independent* if for every database D, and every pair $Consts'$, $Consts''$ such that $(adom(D) \cup adom(Q)) \subseteq Consts', Consts'' \subseteq Consts$, it is the case that $Q_{Consts'}(D) = Q_{Consts''}(D)$. Thus, for an arbitrary database, a domain independent relational calculus query gives the same result regardless of the domain with respect to which is evaluated. In other words, if Q is domain independent, then $Q_{Consts'}(D)$ does not change when $Consts'$ changes. This means that $Q_{Consts'}(D)$ can be computed for $Consts' = adom(D) \cup adom(Q)$.

Example 2.4   Consider the relation schema $R(A, B)$ and the following relational calculus queries:

- $Q^1 = \{(x, y) \mid \exists u \, \exists v \, (R(u, v) \vee R(x, y))\}$;

- $Q^2 = \{(x, y) \mid \neg R(x, y))\}$;

- $Q^3 = \{(x) \mid \forall y R(x, y))\}$.

All the queries above are not domain independent. To see why, consider a relation $r = \{(a, a), (a, b)\}$ and let $Consts'$ be a domain. It is easy to check that $Q^1_{Consts'}(\{r\}) = \{(x, y) \mid x \in Consts' \wedge y \in Consts'\}$ and $Q^2_{Consts'}(\{r\}) = \{(x, y) \mid x \in Consts' \wedge y \in Consts' \wedge (x, y) \notin r\}$. As the results of Q^1 and Q^2 contain values of $Consts'$, then their results clearly depend on $Consts'$. It is easy to see that Q^3 will always contain values taken from the input relation; nevertheless, it is not domain dependent. In fact, it is easy to see that if $Consts'$ is infinite, then $Q^3_{Consts'}(\{r\})$ is empty. The same holds if, for instance, $Consts' = \{a, b, c\}$. However, if $Consts' = \{a, b\}$, then $Q^3_{Consts'}(\{r\}) = \{(a)\}$. Hence, Q^3 can give different results over the same relation when different domains are considered. □

Theorem 2.5 *The problem of deciding whether a relational calculus query is domain independent is undecidable.* □

It is important to observe that the fact that we can express relational calculus queries that are not domain independent is not a positive aspect as, in the presence of an infinite database domain, we can get query answers that have an infinite number of tuples.

In the previous subsection we saw that there does not exist an algorithm to determine whether a relational calculus query is domain independent. We also said that a relational calculus query that is not domain independent is not desirable. Thus, we now present some syntactical restrictions that lead to a class of relational calculus queries, called *safe*, that are guaranteed to be domain independent. Safe relational calculus queries are a subset of the domain independent relational calculus queries.

Safe relational calculus (SRC) is derived from relational calculus by imposing the following restrictions on formulas.

- The universal quantifier ∀ is not used. This does not affect the expressiveness of the language as expressions of the form $\forall x . F$ can be rewritten as $\neg(\exists x . \neg F)$.

- The disjunction operator is applied only to formulas having the same set of free variables.

- For any maximal sub-formula F of the form $F_1 \wedge \cdots \wedge F_n$, all the free variables of F must be *limited* in the following sense:

    - a variable is limited if it is free in some F_i and F_i is not an arithmetic comparison and is not negated;

    - if F_i is of the form $x = c$ or $c = x$, where x is a variable and c is a constant, then x is limited;

    - if F_i is of the form $x = y$ or $y = x$, where x, y are variables and y is limited, then x is limited;

- negation is applied only to an F_i in a maximal sub-formula F of the form $F_1 \wedge \cdots \wedge F_n$ where all free variables are limited.

We use $\mathcal{SRC}$ to denote the set of queries that can be expressed with safe relational calculus.

Theorem 2.6 $\mathcal{RA} = \mathcal{SRC}$. □

2.2.4 DATALOG¬

In this subsection we present another logic based query language for the relational model, namely *Datalog¬* (Datalog with negation).

We assume the existence of a countably infinite set V of variables. Recall that *Consts* is used to denote the database domain. A *literal* is either an atom $R(w_1, \ldots, w_n)$ or a negated atom

$\neg R(w_1, \ldots, w_n)$; in the former case, the literal is said *positive*, whereas in the latter case it is said *negative*. A Datalog⁻ *rule* (or simply rule) r is of the form $A \leftarrow B_1 \wedge \cdots \wedge B_n$, where A is an atom and the B_i's are literals; r is said to be *positive* if every B_i is a positive literal. A is called the *head* of the rule, whereas $B_1 \wedge \cdots \wedge B_n$ is called the *body* of the rule. A Datalog⁻ *program* (or simply program) P is a finite set of rules. A rule (resp. program) is *ground* if no variables occur in it. A ground rule with empty body, that is a rule of the form $A \leftarrow$, is called a *fact*; for notational simplicity we will write it simply as A, that is we drop the arrow. The *definition* of a predicate R in a program P consists of the set of rules in P having R in the head atom. A database can be seen as a finite set of facts. A query can be expressed by means of a program. The set of facts defining a database is called *extensional database*, whereas the set of rules defining a query is called *intensional database*. Predicates are partitioned into *base* and *derived* predicates. Base predicates are those occurring in the extensional database. Derived predicates are those occurring in the intensional database but not in the extensional one. A query Q is a pair (G, P), where G is a predicate and P is a possibly empty program.

The *dependency graph* $\mathcal{G}_P$ of a program P is a directed graph defined as follows: the set of vertices is the set of derived predicates appearing in the program; for each pair of derived predicates R and R' (not necessary different), there is an arc from R to R' iff P contains a rule where R appears in the body and R' appears in the head. Moreover, the arc is labeled with $\neg$ iff P contains a rule where R appears in a negative literal of the body and R' appears in the head. A program P is said to be *recursive* if the dependency graph $\mathcal{G}_P$ is cyclic. Similarly, a derived predicate R is said to be *recursive* if it occurs in a cycle of $\mathcal{G}_P$, whereas two predicates R and R' are *mutually recursive* if they occur in the same cycle.

A program P is said to be: (i) *positive* if all its rules are positive; (ii) *semi-positive* if predicates of negative literals are base predicates; and (iii) *stratified* if the dependency graph does not contain a cycle with an arc labeled with $\neg$.

We now present the semantics of a query $Q = (G, P)$ over a database D. Given a program P, the *Herbrand universe*, denoted $\mathcal{U}_P$, is the set of all constants appearing in P, whereas the *Herbrand base*, denoted $\mathcal{B}_P$, consists of all the ground atoms which can be built using predicates occurring in P and constants in $\mathcal{U}_P$. An interpretation for P is any subset of the Herbrand base $\mathcal{B}_P$. A ground atom A is *true* (resp. *false*) with respect to an interpretation $\mathcal{I}$ if $A \in \mathcal{I}$ (resp. $A \notin \mathcal{I}$). A negative literal $\neg A$ is true with respect to $\mathcal{I}$ if A is false with respect to $\mathcal{I}$. An interpretation $\mathcal{I}$ *satisfies* a ground rule if the atom in the head of the rule is true with respect to $\mathcal{I}$ or at least one literal in the body is false with respect to $\mathcal{I}$. The truth value of empty bodies is assumed to be true, whereas the truth value of empty heads, used to define *denial constraints*, is assumed to be false. The *ground instantiation* of a rule r in P, denoted $ground(r)$, is the set of ground rules obtained from r by replacing every variable with a constant in $\mathcal{U}_P$—with multiple occurrences of the same variable in a rule being replaced with the same constant. The *ground instantiation* of a program P is $ground(P) = \cup_{r \in P} ground(r)$. An interpretation $\mathcal{I}$ is a *model* for P, if $\mathcal{I}$ satisfies every rule in $ground(P)$. A model M for P is *minimal* if there is no model N for P such that $N \subsetneq M$. Every positive program P has a *unique minimal model*, also called *minimum model*, which coincides with the intersection of all models for P.

Example 2.7   Consider the database $D = \{R(a, b), R(b, c)\}$ and the (positive) program P consisting of the following rules:

$$S(x, y) \leftarrow R(x, y)$$
$$S(x, y) \leftarrow R(x, z) \wedge S(z, y) \, .$$

If $P' = P \cup D$, then the Herbrand universe is $\mathcal{U}_{P'} = \{a, b, c\}$, whereas the Herbrand base is $\mathcal{B}_{P'} = \{R(a, a), R(a, b), R(a, c), R(b, a), R(b, b), R(b, c), R(c, a), R(c, b), R(c, c),$ $S(a, a), S(a, b), S(a, c), S(b, a), S(b, b), S(b, c), S(c, a), S(c, b), S(c, c)\}$. The unique minimal model of P' is $\{S(a, b), S(b, c), S(a, c)\} \cup D$. $\square$

The semantics of positive programs is given by the unique. Every semi-positive program has a unique minimal model as well. On the contrary, a stratified program P can have different minimal models, but there is only one minimal model, called the *perfect model*, which captures the intuitive meaning of the program. The perfect model semantics naturally extended the semantics of semi-positive programs, by partitioning the program into subprograms, such that every subprogram defines a maximal set of mutually recursive predicate; subprograms are computed one at the time following the topological order defined by dependencies among predicates. When a subprogram is evaluated, it can be considered a semi-positive programs has predicates non-defined in the current component have been already evaluated and they can be considered as databases facts. More formally, the perfect model of a program P is computed as follows. Let $\mathcal{G}'_P$ be the collapsed graph derived from $\mathcal{G}_P$ by replacing each strongly connected component (i.e., a maximal set of mutually recursive predicates) with a unique node; each node in $\mathcal{G}'_P$ is associated with a sub-program consisting of the rules in P defining predicates in the corresponding component.

Let $\mathcal{G}'_P$ be the collapsed graph derived from $\mathcal{G}_P$, that is $\mathcal{G}'_P$ has one node for each strongly connected component (i.e., a maximal set of mutually recursive predicates) of $\mathcal{G}_P$, while there is an edge (v'_1, v'_2) in $\mathcal{G}'_P$ iff there is an edge (v_1, v_2) in $\mathcal{G}_P$ s.t. v_1 (resp. v_2) is a node of $\mathcal{G}_P$ belonging to the connected component associated with v'_1 (resp. v'_2). Each node in $\mathcal{G}'_P$ is associated with a sub-program consisting of the rules in P defining predicates in the corresponding component. The sub-programs are evaluated one at a time following a topological order of $\mathcal{G}'_P$ (notice that $\mathcal{G}'_P$ is acyclic). It is worth noting that each sub-program can be assumed to be semi-positive as negative literals can be assumed to be base literals as they already have been instantiated.

Example 2.8   Consider the database $D = \{S(a), S(d), T(a), E(a, b), E(b, c), E(c, d)\}$ and the (semi-positive) program P_1 consisting of the rule:

$$R(x) \leftarrow S(x), \neg T(x) \, .$$

The unique minimal model of $P_1 \cup D$ is $D \cup \{R(d)\}$.

Consider now the program P obtained by adding to P_1 the following two rules:

$$Q(x) \leftarrow T(x).$$
$$Q(x) \leftarrow Q(z), \ E(z, x), \ \neg R(x).$$

The dependency graph $\mathcal{G}_P$ consists of the following edges: (Q, Q, ϵ) and $(R, Q, \neg)$, where ϵ in the first edge means that the edge in not labeled and the dependency from Q to itself is positive. The collapsed graph $\mathcal{G}'_P$ consists of two nodes $C_1 = \{R\}$ and $C_2 = \{Q\}$ representing strongly connected components and one edge (C_1, C_2) stating that component C_2 depends on component C_1. Thus, P is partitioned into two subprograms P_1, corresponding to component C_1, and P_2, corresponding to component C_2. Subprogram P_1 consists of the rule defining predicate R, whereas subprogram P_2 consists of the two rules defining predicate Q. The perfect model of P is obtained by first evaluating subprogram P_1 and next subprogram P_2. As said above, the evaluation of P_1 over the database D, that is the evaluation of $P_1 \cup D$, gives the unique minimal model $M_1 = D \cup \{R(d)\}$. Now the subprogram P_2 is evaluated over the database M_1. The program $M_1 \cup P_2$ is semi-positive and has a unique minimal model $M = M_1 \cup \{Q(a), Q(b), Q(c)\}$, which is the perfect model of $P \cup D$. □

As done with relation calculus, in the following we restrict our attention to a restricted subclass of the language.

Safe Datalog$^\neg$ queries are obtained from stratified Datalog$^\neg$ by imposing the restriction that for each rule, every variable must be *limited* in the following sense:

- a variable x is limited if it appears in a positive literal of the body whose predicate symbol is not a comparison operator;

- a variable x is limited if it appears in a comparison operator of the form $x = c$ or $c = x$, where c is a constant;

- a variable x is limited if it appears in a comparison operator of the form $x = y$ or $y = x$, where y is a limited variable.

As an example, a variable appearing only in the head of a rule or only in a negative literal of a rule is not limited. Thus, we say that a rule is *safe* if every variable appearing in it is limited, and a program is *safe* if all its rules are safe.

Example 2.9 The rule $S(x) \leftarrow \neg R(x)$ is not safe. In fact, since x appears in the head and in a negative literal only, then x is not limited. On the contrary, $S(x) \leftarrow R(x) \wedge \neg Q(x)$ is safe. The occurrence of x in $R(x)$ makes x limited; since x is the only variable of the rule, then the rule is safe.

The set of queries that can be expressed by means of non-recursive safe stratified Datalog$^\neg$ programs is denoted by $\mathcal{NR\text{-}SDAT}^\neg$.

Theorem 2.10 $\mathcal{NR\text{-}SDAT}^\neg = \mathcal{SRC} = \mathcal{RA}$.

2.3   CONJUNCTIVE QUERIES

Conjunctive queries are a natural class of queries commonly arising that enjoy different desirable properties (e.g., checking for equivalence and containment of conjunctive queries is decidable). They can be expressed in the languages seen so far as follows.

- Relational calculus: Relational calculus expressions of the form $\{\mathbf{w} \mid \exists \mathbf{x}\, R_1(\mathbf{u}_1) \wedge \cdots \wedge R_k(\mathbf{u}_k)\}$ where $\mathbf{w}$ is a tuple of variables (that must appear in the conjunction) and constants, $\mathbf{x}$ is the tuple of variables in the conjunction that are not in $\mathbf{w}$, the R_i's are relation names, and the $\mathbf{u}_i$'s are tuples of terms (i.e., variables and constants).

- Datalog: Datalog queries expressed by means of non-recursive safe positive Datalog programs where $=$ is the only comparison operator allowed.

- Relational algebra: Relational algebra expressions using only positive selection (i.e., selection conditions are restricted to be conjunctions of equalities), projection, and cartesian product.

BIBLIOGRAPHIC NOTES

Relational model and relational algebra were introduced by Codd [1970]. Relational calculus was introduced in Codd [1972] where the equivalence with relational algebra was addressed as well. Conjunctive queries were first introduced by Chandra and Merlin [1977] and have been deeply investigated in several contexts [Barceló et al., 2012, Cohen et al., 2007, Dalvi and Suciu, 2007, Gottlob et al., 2001, 2006, Johnson and Klug, 1984, Klug, 1988, Kolaitis and Vardi, 2000, Koutris and Suciu, 2011, Wijsen, 2010]. For basic elements of logic programming and deductive databases see [Abiteboul et al., 1995, Lloyd, 1984, Minker, 1988, Ullman, 1988].

For a more complete treatment of relational databases the reader is referred to [Abiteboul et al., 1995, Date, 2000, Elmasri and Navathe, 2000, Garcia-Molina et al., 2009, Maier, 1983, Ramakrishnan and Gehrke, 2003, Silberschatz et al., 2010, Ullman, 1988]

CHAPTER 3

Incomplete Databases

The problem of incomplete information in relational databases have been investigated since the introduction of the relational data model. From a semantic standpoint an *incomplete database* is a set of (complete) databases, also called *possible worlds*. Thus, instead of completely specifying one state of the world, an incomplete database provides a set of alternative possible states of the world.

Different formalisms, called *representation systems*, have been proposed to store a (compact) *representation* of an incomplete database. The focus of this chapter is on representation systems based on *null values*, although other approaches not relying on null values have been proposed to represent an incomplete database. Different kinds of null values have been investigated over the years: an *unknown* null indicates that a value exists but is not known, an *inapplicable* (or *non-existing*) null specifies that a value does not exist, a *no-information* null indicates that we do not know whether a value exists or not.

3.1 INCOMPLETE DATABASES

An incomplete database simply is a set of complete databases (called *possible worlds*). As an incomplete database provides different possible states of the real world, a query may return a set of answers for each possible world.

Definition 3.1 Given a query Q and an incomplete database I, the result of evaluating Q over I is $Q(I) = \{Q(D) \mid D \in I\}$.

Thus, $Q(I)$ contains a set of query answers for each possible world of I. Nevertheless, there may be some tuples that are answers to Q no matter what possible world happens to be the true state of the real world. On the other hand, there may be tuples that are answers to Q with respect to some, but not necessarily every, possible world. These considerations lead to the notions of *certain* and *possible* query answers. A tuple is a *certain* answer to a query Q with respect to an incomplete database I if it is an answer to Q in every possible world of I.

Definition 3.2 The set of *certain answers* to a query Q with respect to an incomplete database I is defined as follows:

$$certain(Q, I) = \bigcap_{D \in I} Q(D) .$$

A tuple is a *possible* answer to Q with respect to I if it is an answer to Q in some possible world of I.

Definition 3.3   The set of *possible answers* to a query Q with respect to an incomplete database I is defined as follows:

$$possible(Q, I) = \bigcup_{D \in I} Q(D) .$$

3.2   REPRESENTATION SYSTEMS

Several approaches (called *representation systems*) have been proposed to represent incomplete databases in a compact way. In the following, we present representation systems based on (unknown) null values. They essentially extend the relational model by allowing labeled nulls to appear in tuples; the represented possible worlds are those complete databases that can be obtained by replacing all the labeled nulls with constants—indeed, some representation systems such as c-tables (that will be presented in the following) allow one to specify some restrictions on how nulls can be replaced. We also recall the important notions of a *strong* and *weak* representation system, and give a picture of how the different representation systems behave with respect to such properties.

We start by introducing some notation and terminology that will be used in the following. We assume the existence of a countably infinite set $Nulls = \{\eta_i \mid i \in \mathbb{N}\}$ of *labeled nulls*. Recall that $\mathcal{D}$ denotes the database domain. A *valuation* is a mapping $v : Nulls \cup \mathcal{D} \to \mathcal{D}$, such that $v(c) = c$ for every $c \in \mathcal{D}$. Hence, a valuation maps every constant to itself and every labeled null to a constant. The result of applying a valuation v over a tuple t (resp. relation r, database D) possibly containing labeled nulls is denoted by $v(t)$ (resp. $v(r)$, $v(D)$) and is defined in the natural fashion (e.g., $v(t)$ is the tuple obtained from t by replacing every occurrence of a labeled null η_i with $v(\eta_i)$).

Given a representation T (in some representation system) of an incomplete database, we use $rep(T)$ to denote the set of complete databases represented by T (or, in other words, by the incomplete database represented by T). Given a query Q, we would always like to be able to find a representation of the answers to Q over the incomplete database represented by T, using the same representation system of T. More precisely, for each query Q and representation T of an incomplete database, we would like to compute a representation T' (from T and Q) such that $rep(T') = Q(rep(T))$. If a representation system has this property for a query language $\mathcal{L}$ then it is said to be a *strong* representation system for $\mathcal{L}$. The following commutative diagram illustrates this point.

$$
\begin{array}{ccc}
T & \xrightarrow{\ rep\ } & rep(T) \\
\downarrow Q & & \downarrow Q \\
T' & \xrightarrow{\ rep\ } & Q(rep(T))
\end{array}
$$

We now present the notion of a *weak* representation system by relaxing the requirements of a strong representation system.

Given a query language $\mathcal{L}$, we say that two incomplete databases I and I' are *$\mathcal{L}$-equivalent*, denoted $I \equiv_{\mathcal{L}} I'$, if $certain(Q, I) = certain(Q, I')$ for each query Q of $\mathcal{L}$. A representation system is *weak* for a query language $\mathcal{L}$ if for each representation T of an incomplete database and query Q of $\mathcal{L}$ there exists a representation T' such that $rep(T') \equiv_{\mathcal{L}} Q(rep(T))$. As opposed to a strong representation system, a weak representation system is not required to be able to represent $Q(rep(T))$ for every query Q and representation T; however, a weak representation system must be able to provide a representation T' s.t. $rep(T')$ is $\mathcal{L}$-equivalent to $Q(rep(T))$—this means that $rep(T')$ and $Q(rep(T))$ are indistinguishable as long as we are interested only in the certain answers to queries in $\mathcal{L}$.

In the following, different representation systems are presented. To simplify the presentation, we restrict our discussion to unirelational databases, and assume that every attribute domain coincides with the database domain $\mathcal{D}$. Generalization is straightforward.

Codd tables A *Codd table* is a relation possibly containing labeled nulls from *Nulls*, where each labeled null can occur at most once. The incomplete database represented by a Codd table T is defined as follows:

$$rep(T) = \{v(T) \mid v \text{ is a valuation}\} .$$

Thus, the possible worlds represented by T are the complete databases that can be derived from T by replacing every labeled null in T with a constant. It is important to highlight that the previous definition of $rep(T)$ assumes the Closed World Assumption (CWA) because each tuple in a possible world of $rep(T)$ must be derived from a tuple of T. If the Open World Assumption (OWA) is made, then the possible worlds represented by T include $rep(T)$ and any other complete database that contains a database in $rep(T)$.

Example 3.4 Assume $\eta_1, \eta_2, \eta_3, \eta_4$ are labeled nulls in *Nulls*. The following is a Codd table:

A	B	C
0	1	η_1
η_2	η_3	1
2	0	η_4

The following relations are some of the possible worlds represented by the previous Codd table:

A	B	C
0	1	1
1	1	1
2	0	2

A	B	C
0	1	2
1	2	1
2	0	1

A	B	C
0	1	2
4	2	1
2	0	0

As an example, the first relation above is obtained from the Codd table by means of a valuation v s.t. $v(\eta_1) = 1, v(\eta_2) = 1, v(\eta_3) = 1, v(\eta_4) = 2$. Under the OWA, the following is also one of the possible worlds (because it is a superset of the first possible world reported above):

A	B	C
0	1	1
1	1	1
2	0	2
1	1	0

As illustrated in the following example, Codd tables are not a strong representation system even for very restricted subsets of relational algebra.

Example 3.5   To give an idea of why Codd tables fail to be a strong representation system for different subsets of relational algebra, consider the Codd table of Example 3.4, call it T, and the simple query Q defined as $\sigma_{A=4}(T)$. Clearly, $Q(rep(T))$ contains an empty relation (this is obtained, for instance, by evaluating Q over the first possible world reported in Example 3.4) and at least one non-empty relation (e.g., the one obtained by evaluating Q over the third possible world reported in Example 3.4). It can be easily verified that there is no Codd table T' whose possible worlds contain the two aforementioned relations.

Codd Tables form a weak representation system for the subset of relational algebra consisting only of selection (involving equalities and inequalities) and projection. If we consider a language that allows also join or union, then Codd tables are no longer a weak representation system for such a language.

Naive tables   One of the limitations of Codd tables is that a labeled null can occur at most once. *Naive tables* remove this limitation and are defined like Codd tables except that labeled nulls are allowed to occur more than once.[1]

The set of possible worlds represented by a naive table T is defined in the same way as done for Codd tables, namely:

$$rep(T) = \{v(T) \mid v \text{ is a valuation}\}.$$

Notice that if a naive table contains multiple occurrences of the same labeled null, then possible worlds are obtained by replacing the different occurrences of the same labeled null with the same constant.

Example 3.6   Assume η_1, η_2, η_3 are labeled nulls in *Nulls*. The following is a naive table (but not a Codd table because of the two occurrences of η_1):

---

[1]Naive tables have also been called *V-tables* and *e-tables* [Abiteboul and Grahne, 1985, Grahne, 1984, Imielinski and Lipski, 1984].

A	B	C
0	1	η_1
η_2	η_3	1
2	0	η_1

Notice that the naive table above says that even if the C-values of the first and third tuples are unknown, we know that they are the same.

The following relations are some of the possible worlds represented by the previous naive table:

A	B	C
0	1	1
1	1	1
2	0	1

A	B	C
0	1	2
1	2	1
2	0	2

A	B	C
0	1	2
3	2	1
2	0	2

As an example, the first relation above is obtained from the naive table by means of a valuation v s.t. $v(\eta_1) = 1, v(\eta_2) = 1, v(\eta_3) = 1$. We remark again that for each possible world of the previous naive table the C-value of the first tuple is equal to the C-value of the third tuple.

Naive tables are a weak representation system for relational algebra queries using selection (where only equalities are allowed), projection, join and union. For a query Q in this class, the certain answers to Q with respect to the incomplete database represented by a naive table T can be computed as follows: first, Q is evaluated over T in the standard way by treating labeled nulls as new constants different from any constant in the database domain; then, tuples in the result containing labeled nulls are discarded and the remaining tuples are the certain answers.

Conditional tables So far we have seen that neither Codd nor naive tables are a strong representation system for full relational algebra. We now present a much more powerful representation system, namely *conditional tables*, that forms a strong representation system for relational algebra.

A *condition* is a conjunction of atoms of the form $\eta_i = \eta_j, \eta_i = c, \eta_i \neq \eta_j,$ or $\eta_i \neq c,$ where η_i and η_j are labeled nulls and c is a constant. A valuation v *satisfies* a condition ϕ iff by replacing every occurrence of labeled null η_i in ϕ with $v(\eta_i)$, the resulting formula is true. A *conditional table* (*c-table* for short) is a triple $\langle T, \Phi, \Psi \rangle$ where T is a naive table, Φ is a condition (called *global condition*) and Ψ is a function mapping every tuple of T to a condition (conditions associated with tuples via function Ψ are called *local conditions*). Global and local conditions can contain labeled nulls not appearing in T.

The set of possible worlds represented by a conditional table $\langle T, \Phi, \Psi \rangle$ is defined as follows:

$$rep(\langle T, \Phi, \Psi \rangle) = \{r \mid \text{ there exists a valuation } v \text{ such that}$$
$$v \text{ satisfies } \Phi \text{ and } r = \{v(t) \mid t \in T \text{ and } v \text{ satisfies } \Psi(t)\}\} .$$

Notice that the previous definition of *rep* adopts the closed world assumption.

Example 3.7   Suppose we know that Sally is taking math or computer science (CS), but not both, and another course that is not known. Alice takes biology if Sally takes math, and math or physics, but not both, if Sally takes physics. This can be represented by the following c-table.

$$\eta_1 \neq math \wedge \eta_1 \neq CS$$

Student	Course	
Sally	math	$\eta_2 = 0$
Sally	CS	$\eta_2 \neq 0$
Sally	η_1	
Alice	biology	$\eta_2 = 0$
Alice	math	$\eta_1 = physics \wedge \eta_3 = 0$
Alice	physics	$\eta_1 = physics \wedge \eta_3 \neq 0$

In the previous c-table η_1, η_2, and η_3 are labeled nulls. The global condition Φ is $\eta_1 \neq math \wedge \eta_1 \neq CS$. For each tuple the condition associated by Ψ is reported in the last column (a missing condition for a tuple t means that $\Psi(t) = true$).

The following relations are some of the possible worlds represented by the previous c-table.

Student	Course
Sally	math
Sally	physics
Alice	biology
Alice	math

Student	Course
Sally	math
Sally	biology
Alice	biology

Student	Course
Sally	CS
Sally	biology

As an example, the first relation above is obtained from the c-table by means of a valuation v s.t. $v(\eta_1) = physics$, $v(\eta_2) = 0$, $v(\eta_3) = 0$.

A valuation v such that $v(\eta_1) = math$, $v(\eta_2) = 1$ would lead to the following relation.

Student	Course
Sally	CS
Sally	math

However, this relation is not a possible world because v does not satisfy the global condition.

c-tables form a strong representation for relational algebra.

Horn tables   A *Horn table* is a c-table where conditions are of a restricted form. More precisely, *Horn conditions* are of the following form:

- $\eta_i = c$ and $\eta_i = \eta_j$ are (atomic) Horn conditions—here η_i and η_j are labeled nulls whereas c is a constant;

- $\neg C_1 \vee \cdots \vee \neg C_n$ is a Horn condition—here the C_i's are atomic Horn conditions;

- $C_1 \wedge \cdots \wedge C_n \to C_{n+1}$ is a Horn condition—here the C_i's are atomic Horn conditions.

A c-table is a Horn table if the global condition is a Horn condition and local conditions are of the form $C_1 \wedge \cdots \wedge C_n$, where the C_i's are atomic Horn conditions.

Example 3.8   The c-table of Example 3.7 is not a Horn table. One reason is that the global condition is not Horn. Furthermore, the local conditions of the second and last tuple are not Horn.

Property of tables   From the discussion above it is clear that Codd tables are naive tables and naive tables are Horn tables (furthermore, as already mentioned, Horn tables are a restricted class of c-tables).

The following table gives a summary of the query languages with respect to which each representation system is strong and weak. Each language is a (not necessarily strict) subset of relational algebra and is denoted by the letters indicating the relational algebra operators allowed by the language: P (resp. S, S$^+$, U, J, R, D) denotes projection (resp. selection, selection with only equalities allowed, union, join, renaming, difference).

Table class	Strong representation system	Weak representation system
C-tables	PSUJRD	PSUJRD
Horn tables	PS$^+$UJR	PS$^+$UJR
Naive tables	PUR	PS$^+$UJR
Codd tables	PR	PSR

3.3   NULLS IN SQL

The SQL standard provides one single constant NULL to represent a missing value. Generally, the full behavior of the NULL value in SQL is not described in detail, as the SQL rules surrounding NULL can be ambiguous, often not intuitive and in some case surprising. How NULLs should be handled in SQL, in all circumstances, is not clear from the standard documents.

In SQL, a NULL indicates that the value is unknown. Notice that a NULL occurrence is different from the value zero, the empty string, and even from other NULL occurrences, that is two occurrences of NULL are not equal. Indeed, any comparison between a NULL and any other value—a constant or another NULL—yields the *unknown* truth value because the value of a NULL is unknown. Thus, in the presence of NULLs, SQL considers a three-valued logic where the truth values are $false, unknown,$ and $true$. As an example, given two relations, $r_1 = \{(a, NULL), (b, 1), (c, 2)\}$ and $r_2 = \{(a, NULL)\}$ with schemas $R_1(A, B)$ and $R_2(C, D)$, the join of r_1 and r_2 with join condition $B = D$ gives in output an empty relation, while the union of r_1 and r_2 is equal to $\{(a, NULL), (b, 1), (c, 2)\}$. Moreover, the selection of the tuples of r_1 satisfying the condition $B = 1$ gives the relation $\{(b, 1)\}$, whereas if the condition is $B \neq 1$ we get the relation $\{(c, 2)\}$, as *NULL* cannot be assumed to be equal to 1, but cannot even be assumed to be different from 1, hence both comparisons yield the truth value *unknown* and the first tuple of r_1 is not included in the result. In fact, only tuples for which the comparison yields *true* are included in the result.

Under the linear ordering $false < unknown < true$ defined over the truth values, the meaning of the logical operators $\wedge$ and $\vee$ does not change as $A \wedge B = min\{A, B\}$ and $A \vee B = max\{A, B\}$; the meaning of the negation operators must be extended assuming that $\neg unknown = unknown$ is true. Moreover, arithmetic operators involving NULLs give as result a NULL. Although it is reasonable that $NULL + 5 = NULL$, surprisingly $NULL \times 0 = NULL$. More surprisingly is the fact that in SQL if we count the tuples in the above relation r_1 the result is 3 (SELECT COUNT(*) FROM R_1), but if we count the tuples in the relation obtained by projecting r_1 over attribute B the result is 2 (SELECT COUNT(B) FROM R_1) and if we sum the values in the second column of r_1 the result is 3 (SELECT SUM(B) FROM R_1).

BIBLIOGRAPHIC NOTES

In this chapter we presented a number of representation systems that extend the relational model by allowing variables (denoting unknown null values) to occur in the database. Some of the material of this chapter has been taken from the excellent books of Grahne [1991] and Abiteboul et al. [1995].

Databases containing null values have been investigated since the beginning of the relational data model [Atzeni and Morfuni, 1986, Biskup, 1979, Codd, 1979, Grant, 1977, Imielinski and Lipski, 1981, 1984, Levene and Loizou, 1999, Lien, 1982, Lipski, 1979, Zaniolo, 1984]. It was recognized early on that there are different types of null values, each of which reflects different intuitions about why a particular piece of information is missing.

No-information nulls were introduced by Zaniolo [1984] to deal with the case where it is not known whether a missing value exists or not. They have also been considered by Atzeni and Morfuni [1986], Hartmann and Link [2010, 2012], Hartmann et al. [2012], Lien [1982], where the problem of dealing with integrity constraints in the presence of no-information nulls is studied.

A greater amount of work has been devoted to the study of databases containing only unknown nulls. In this context, different problems have been addressed, such as query answering [Abiteboul et al., 1991, Grahne, 1991, Lipski, 1984, Reiter, 1986, Yuan and Chiang, 1988], the characterization of consistency in the presence of integrity constraints [Grahne, 1991, Imielinski and Lipski, 1983, Levene and Loizou, 1998, 1999, Vassiliou, 1980], and updating the database [Abiteboul and Grahne, 1985, Grahne, 1991]. More expressive data models where the values that (labeled) unknown nulls can take can be constrained were considered by Abiteboul et al. [1991], Grahne [1991], Imielinski and Lipski [1984].

Other formalisms (not necessarily relying on null values) to represent incomplete databases have been proposed over the years. A way of representing incomplete databases akin to the representation systems seen in this chapter has been considered by Imielinski et al. [1995], where *OR-databases* are introduced. Similar to the tables discussed in this chapter, OR-databases allow variables (called *OR-objects*) to occur in the database; however, the domain of each variable is *finite*. Antova et al.

[2009] present the notion of *world-set decompositions* (WSDs), a decomposition-based approach to represent any finite set of possible worlds. Sarma et al. [2009] study a space of models to represent a finite set of possible worlds. The most general of these models allows constants and finite sets of alternative constants to occur in a relation; in addition, each relation is associated with a boolean formula built from tuple identifiers.

In Bertossi and Li [2011], in applications to data privacy a single null is used, with a semantics that follows a reconstruction in first-order predicate logic of null in SQL databases. A first version of that semantics was used in Bertossi and Bravo [2007], Bravo and Bertossi [2006].

A formal semantics for SQL null values that exactly captures the behaviors of SQL queries and SQL constraints in the presence of null values has been proposed in Franconi and Tessaris [2012a,b].

CHAPTER 4

The Chase Algorithm

The Chase is a fixpoint algorithm enforcing satisfaction of data dependencies in databases. It was proposed more than 30 years ago by Aho et al. [1979a], Maier et al. [1979] and has received increasing attention in recent years in both database theory and practical applications.

The execution of the chase algorithm involves the insertion of tuples with possible null values, and the changing of null values, which can be made equal to constants or other null values. However, the insertion of tuples with new (null) values could result in a non-terminating execution.

4.1 DATA DEPENDENCIES

An *embedded dependency* is a first-order logic sentence of the form:

$$\forall \mathbf{x} \, \forall \mathbf{y} \, \phi(\mathbf{x}, \mathbf{y}) \rightarrow \exists \mathbf{z} \, \psi(\mathbf{x}, \mathbf{z}) \,, \tag{4.1}$$

where $\mathbf{x}, \mathbf{y}, \mathbf{z}$ are tuple of variables, $\phi(\mathbf{x}, \mathbf{y})$ and $\psi(\mathbf{x}, \mathbf{z})$ are conjunctions of atoms (relation and equality atoms), called the *body* and the *head* of the dependency, respectively. Without loss of generality, we assume that equality atoms may appear only in the head of the dependency and there is no existentially quantified variable involved in an equality atom.

Subclasses of embedded dependencies are:

- *unirelational* dependencies: only one relational symbol is used in ϕ and ψ;

- *1-head* dependencies: only a single atom in the head;

- *tuple generating* dependencies (TGDs): no equality atoms;

- *full* dependencies: no existentially quantified variables $\mathbf{z}$;

- *equality generating* dependencies (EGDs): full, 1-head with an equality atom in the head;

Recall that a database D can be seen as a finite set of facts. We say that D *satisfies* (or is *consistent* with respect to) a dependency σ if $D \models \sigma$ in the standard model-theoretic sense. D *satisfies* (or is *consistent* with respect to) a set of dependency Σ iff D satisfies every dependency in Σ.

4.2   UNIVERSAL SOLUTIONS AND QUERY ANSWERS

For any database instance D and set of dependencies Σ over the same database schema, a *solution* for (D, Σ) is an instance J such that $D \subseteq J$ and $J \models \Sigma$ (i.e. J satisfies all the dependencies in Σ). The set of solutions for (D, Σ) will be denoted by $Sol(D, \Sigma)$.

Definition 4.1 (Homomorphism)   Let K and J be two instances over the same database schema with values in $Consts \cup Nulls$. A *homomorphism* $h : K \to J$ is a mapping from $Consts(K) \cup Nulls(K)$ to $Consts(J) \cup Nulls(J)$ such that: (1) $h(c) = c$, for every $c \in Consts(K)$, and (2) for every fact $R_i(t)$ of K, we have that $R_i(h(t))$ is a fact of J (where, if $t = (a_1, ..., a_s)$, then $h(t) = (h(a_1), ..., h(a_s)))$.

J and K are said to be *homomorphically equivalent* if there is a homomorphism $h : K \to J$ and a homomorphism $h' : J \to K$. $\square$

Similar to homomorphisms between instances, a homomorphism h from a formula $\rho(\mathbf{x})$, denoting either a conjunctive formula or a data dependency, to an instance J is a mapping from the variables $\mathbf{x}$ appearing in the formula to $Consts(J) \cup Nulls(J)$, such that for every atom $R(x_1, ..., x_n)$ of $\phi(\mathbf{x})$ the fact $R(h(x_1), ..., h(x_n))$ is in J. The application of homomorphism h to $\rho(\mathbf{x})$), denoted by $h(\rho(\mathbf{x}))$, consists in the replacement of variables in $\mathbf{x}$ with values in $Consts(J) \cup Nulls(J)$, as defined in h.

Example 4.2   Consider the three databases $D_1 = \{R(a, b), R(a, \eta_1)\}$, $D_2 = \{R(a, b)\}$ and $D_3 = \{R(a, b), R(a, d)\}$. D_1 and D_2 are homomorphically equivalent as there are two homomorphisms $h_1 = \{\eta_1/b\}$ and $h_2 = \{\}$ such that $h_1(D_1) \subseteq D_2$ and $h_2(D_2) \subseteq D_1$. Although there is an homomorphism from D_1 to D_3 ($h_3 = \{\eta_1/d\}$ and $h_3(D_1) \subseteq D_3$) D_1 and D_3 are not homomorphically equivalent as there is no homomorphism from D_3 to D_1.

Consider now the conjunctive formula $\phi = R(x, y) \wedge R(x, z)$. There is, for instance, an homomorphism h from ϕ to D_1 (namely $h = \{x/a, y/b, z/\eta_1\}$. $\square$

A *universal solution* J is a solution such that for every solution J' there exists a homomorphism $h : J \to J'$. The set of universal solutions for (D, Σ) will be denoted by $USol(D, \Sigma)$. The next proposition states that universal solutions are homomorphically equivalent.

Proposition 4.3   [Fagin et al., 2005a] *Let Σ be a set of data dependencies defined over a given database schema. Then:*

- *for any database D, if J and K are universal solutions for D and Σ, then J and K are homomorphically equivalent;*

- *for any pair of database instances D_1 and D_2, such that J_1 and J_2 are universal solutions for (D_1, Σ) and (D_2, Σ), respectively, J_1 and J_2 are homomorphically equivalent if and only if $Sol(D_1, \Sigma) = Sol(D_2, \Sigma)$.* $\square$

Therefore, universal solutions are unique up to homomorphic equivalence, and each of them embodies the space of solutions. The problem of checking whether universal solutions exist and how to compute them have been recently investigated. In particular, as we shall see next, it has been shown that the chase algorithm can be used to compute universal solutions and that every finite chase, if it does not fail, computes a (*canonical*) universal solution. If the chase fails, then no solution exists.

A homomorphism $h : K \rightarrow J$ such that $J \subseteq K$ and $h(x) = x$ for each x in J is called *retraction* and J is called a *retraction of K*. A retraction is *proper* if it is not surjective. An instance is a *core* if it has no proper retractions. A *core of an instance K*, denoted as $core(K)$, is a retraction of K which is a core. Cores of an instance K are unique up to isomorphism. Considering Example 4.2, homomorphism h_1 from D_1 to D_2 is a retraction as $D_2 \subseteq D_1$ and $h(x) = x$ for each x in D_2 (D_2 is a retraction of D_1). Databases D_2 and D_3 are cores as, being grounded, there is no retraction for them.

All universal solutions have the same core (up to isomorphism) which is the smallest universal solution. The complexity and the efficient computation of the core of a universal solution has been studied [Fagin et al., 2005b, Gottlob and Nash, 2008]. Methods for directly computing the core by SQL queries in a data exchange framework where schema mappings are specified by source-to-target TGDs have been developed [Mecca et al., 2009, ten Cate et al., 2009].

Query answering

Definition 4.4   The set of certain answers to a query Q over a database D with data dependencies Σ is

$$certain(Q, D, \Sigma) = \bigcap \{q(J) \mid J \in Sol(D, \Sigma)\} \, .$$

For any set of tuples S with null values, $S_\downarrow$ consists of the tuples in S containing only constants.

Proposition 4.5   [Fagin et al., 2005a] *Let D be a database and Σ a set of data dependencies over a given schema. Then:*

- *for every union of conjunctive queries Q, $certain(Q, D, \Sigma) = Q(J)_\downarrow$, where J is a universal solution for D and Σ;*

- *if there is a database J such that, for every conjunctive query Q, $certain(Q, D, \Sigma) = Q(J)$, then J is a universal solution for D and Σ.*   □

4.3   DEPENDENCY SKOLEMIZATION

Given a TGD r of the form (4.1) we denote with

$$sk(r) : \forall \mathbf{x} \, \forall \mathbf{z} \, \phi(\mathbf{x}, \mathbf{z}) \to \psi(\mathbf{x}, sk(\mathbf{y}))$$

the skolemized version of r, where each existentially quantified variable $y_i \in \mathbf{y}$ is replaced by a skolem term $f_{y_i}^r(\mathbf{w})$ where $f_{y_i}^r$ is a skolem function and $\mathbf{w}$ denotes the set of universally quantified variables in r defining the scope of the variables $\mathbf{y}$[1]. In order to clearly identify universally quantified variables denoting the scope of existentially quantified variables we use parenthesis. For instance, in a TGD r of the form

$$\forall \mathbf{x} \, (\forall \mathbf{z} \, \phi(\mathbf{x}, \mathbf{z}) \to \exists y_1, ..., y_n \psi(\mathbf{x}, y_1, ..., y_n))$$

variables in $\mathbf{x}$ denote the scope of existentially quantified variables and, therefore, $sk(r)$ (obtained after the rewriting of r in prenex normal form, the skolemization of existentially quantified variables and the re-rewriting of the dependency with the implication operator) is equal to

$$\forall \mathbf{x} \, (\forall \mathbf{z} \, \phi(\mathbf{x}, \mathbf{z}) \to \psi(\mathbf{x}, f_{y_1}^r(\mathbf{x}), ..., f_{y_n}^r(\mathbf{x}))),$$

whereas if r is of the form

$$\forall \mathbf{x} \, \forall \mathbf{z} \, (\phi(\mathbf{x}, \mathbf{z}) \to \exists y_1, ..., y_n \psi(\mathbf{x}, y_1, ..., y_n))$$

the corresponding skolemized dependency $sk(r)$ is equal to

$$\forall \mathbf{x} \, \forall \mathbf{z} \, (\phi(\mathbf{x}, \mathbf{z}) \to \psi(\mathbf{x}, f_{y_1}^r(\mathbf{x}, \mathbf{z}), ..., f_{y_n}^r(\mathbf{x}, \mathbf{z}))).$$

For instance, the skolemized version of the TGD $r = \forall x \, (\forall z \, R(x, z) \to \exists y \, S(x, y))$ is $sk(r) = \forall x \, (\forall z \, R(x, z) \to S(x, f_y^r(x)))$, whereas the skolemized version of the TGD $s = \forall x \, \forall z \, (R(x, z) \to \exists y \, S(x, y))$ is $sk(r) = \forall x \, (\forall z \, R(x, z) \to S(x, f_y^s(x, z)))$. Basically, universally quantified variable z in r is interpreted as existentially quantified, that is r is equivalent to the TGD $\forall x \, \exists z \, R(x, z) \to \exists y \, S(x, y)$; in such a case parenthesis used to separate universal and existential variables can be omitted. For a full data dependency r (including EGDs), $sk(r) = r$. The skolemized version of a set Σ of dependencies is $sk(\Sigma) = \{sk(r) \mid r \in \Sigma\}$. Since $sk(\Sigma)$ is satisfiable if and only if the original set Σ is satisfiable, the database D and the set of dependencies Σ admit a "solution" if and only if D and $sk(\Sigma)$ admit a solution.

4.4   STANDARD CHASE ALGORITHM

If a data dependency is not satisfied by a database instance, it is possible to "repair" the database instance by extending it with new atoms, or by renaming nulls values. The procedure that enforces the validity of a set of data dependencies is called the *chase*.

---

[1]If the set of variables $\mathbf{w}$ is empty, then the skolem function of arity 0 results in a skolem constant.

Depending on when or how a chase step is applied, different chase variations have been considered [Cali et al., 2008, Deutsch et al., 2008, Fagin et al., 2005a, Marnette, 2009, Meier et al., 2009a, ten Cate et al., 2009]. To differentiate between the variations of the chase procedure we will call the chase procedure considered by Fagin et al. [2005a] for the data exchange problem the *standard chase*.

In the following we will often omit quantifications, since we assume that variables appearing in the body are universally quantified and variables appearing only in the head are existentially quantified.

Definition 4.6   (Standard Chase Step)   [Fagin et al., 2005a] Let K be a database instance.

1. Let r be a TGD $\phi(\mathbf{x}, \mathbf{z}) \to \exists \mathbf{y} \, \psi(\mathbf{x}, \mathbf{y})$. Let h be a homomorphism from $\phi(\mathbf{x}, \mathbf{z})$ to K such that there is no extension of h to a homomorphism h' from $\phi(\mathbf{x}, \mathbf{z}) \wedge \psi(\mathbf{x}, \mathbf{y})$ to K . We say that r can be *applied* to K with homomorphism h. Let K' be the union of K with the set of facts obtained by: (a) extending h to h' such that each variable in $\mathbf{y}$ is assigned a fresh labeled null, followed by (b) taking the image of the atoms of ψ under h'. We say that the result of applying r to K with h is K', and write $K \overset{r,h}{\to} K'$.

2. Let r be an EGD $\phi(\mathbf{x}) \to x_1 = x_2$. Let h be a homomorphism from $\phi(\mathbf{x})$ to K such that $h(x_1) \neq h(x_2)$. We say that r can be *applied* to K with homomorphism h. More specifically, we distinguish two cases.

   (a) If both $h(x_1)$ and $h(x_2)$ are in $Consts$ the result of applying r to K with h is "failure", and write $K \overset{r,h}{\to} \perp$.

   (b) Otherwise, let K' be K where we identify $h(x_1)$ and $h(x_2)$ as follows: if one is a constant, then the labeled null is replaced everywhere by the constant; if both are labeled nulls, then one is replaced everywhere by the other. We say that the result of applying r to K with h is K', and write $K \overset{r,h}{\to} K'$.   □

Definition 4.7   (Standard Chase)   [Fagin et al., 2005a] Let Σ be a set of TGDs and EGDs, and let K be an instance.

- A *chase sequence of K with Σ* is a (finite or infinite) sequence of chase steps $K_i \overset{r_i,h_i}{\to} K_{i+1}$, with $i = 0, 1, ..., K_0 = K$ and r_i a dependency in Σ.

- A *finite chase of K with Σ* is a finite chase sequence $K_i \overset{r_i,h_i}{\to} K_{i+1}, 0 \leq i < m$, with the requirement that either (a) $K_m = \perp$, or (b) there is no dependency r_m of Σ and there is no homomorphism h_m such that r_m can be applied to K_m with h_m. We say that K_m is the result of the finite chase. We refer to case (a) as the case of a *failing finite chase* and we refer to case (b) as the case of a *successful finite chase*.   □

The chase of an instance K with respect to a set of dependencies Σ, denoted by $chase(\Sigma, K)$, is the (finite or infinite) instance obtained by applying all applicable chase steps exhaustively to K. Observe that the definition of chase sequence is non-deterministic, as it does not impose any condition on the choice of an applicable dependency during a chase step.

Example 4.8   Consider the following set of TGDs $\Sigma_{4.8}$:

$$r_1 : R(x) \to Q(x)$$
$$r_2 : P(x) \to Q(y)$$

and the database $D = \{R(a), P(a)\}$. Both r_1 and r_2 are applicable to D. If we choose to apply r_1, we have $D \xrightarrow{r_1, h_1} D_1 = \{R(a), P(a), Q(a)\}$ and $D_1 \models \Sigma_{4.8}$. Alternatively, if we choose to apply r_2, we have $D \xrightarrow{r_2, h_2} D_2 = \{R(a), P(a), Q(\eta_1)\}$ and $D_2 \not\models r_1$; thus we have to apply r_1 to D_2, obtaining $D_2 \xrightarrow{r_1, h'_1} D_{21} = \{R(a), P(a), Q(\eta_1), Q(a)\}$ and $D_{21} \models \Sigma_{4.8}$. Both D_1 and D_{21} are universal solutions. □

The chase non-determinism makes the chase process to be viewed as a tree, namely the *chase execution tree*, where level i in the tree represents the i-th step in the chase algorithm and where to each node a new edge is added for each of the applicable dependencies. Each path from the root of the tree to a leaf node represents an *(execution) branch*. Consequently, as in the situation above, the algorithm may return different instances depending on the branch considered. The following theorem states that universal solutions can be computed using the chase algorithm.

Theorem 4.9   [Fagin et al., 2005a] *Let D be a database and Σ a set of data dependencies over a given schema. Then:*

- *if J is the result of some successful finite chase of (Σ, D), then J is a (canonical) universal solution; and*

- *if some failing finite chase of (Σ, D) exists, then does not exist any solution.*   □

The previous theorem states that if there is a failing sequence of (Σ, D), then all sequences are not successful, but this does not mean that all sequences are failing. Symmetrically, if there is a successful sequence, then all sequences are not failing. Indeed, it may happen that some branches lead to finite instances, whereas others to infinite instances.

Example 4.10   Consider the following set of TGDs $\Sigma_{4.10}$:

$$r_1 : R(x, y, z) \to \exists w \, R(x, z, w)$$
$$r_2 : R(x, y, z) \wedge R(x, y_1, z_1) \to z = z_1$$

Given a database D such that $D \not\models r_1$ and $D \models r_2$ (e.g., $D = \{R(a, b, c)\}$), the chase sequence that never fires r_2 is infinite, while every chase sequence that fires r_1 a finite number of times and then only fires r_2 is finite and satisfies $\Sigma_{4.10}$. More generally, all finite chase sequences are successful, but there are infinite chase sequences as well. Analogously, given a null-free database D', such that $D' \not\models r_1$ and $D' \not\models r_2$ (e.g., $D' = \{R(a, b, c), R(a, c, d)\}$), the chase sequence that never fires r_2 is infinite, while every chase sequence that fires r_1 a finite number of times and then only fires r_2 is finite and failing. For such a database we have that all finite chase sequences are successful, but there are infinite chase sequences as well. □

Theorem 4.11 [Deutsch et al., 2008] *Consider an instance J and a set Σ of TGDs.*

1. *It is undecidable whether some chase sequence of J with Σ terminates.*

2. *It is undecidable whether all chase sequences of J with Σ terminate.*

The undecidability holds even over a fixed schema, and even if J is an empty instance. □

Because of the undecidability of the chase termination problem, several sufficient criteria and techniques have been defined to ensure the termination of the algorithm (see Chapter 5).

4.5 OBLIVIOUS CHASE

Besides the standard chase, another kind of chase procedure, known as *oblivious chase*, has been considered. Intuitively, a standard chase step applies only when there exists a mapping from the body of a dependency to the database instance and the head of the dependency is not satisfied, while an oblivious one always applies when there exists a mapping from the body to the instance, even if the dependency is satisfied. Two different types of oblivious chase algorithms have been used in the literature: *oblivious naive* [Cali et al., 2008, Meier et al., 2009a, ten Cate et al., 2009] and *oblivious skolem* [Marnette, 2009]. Before defining these chase variants, we explain their differences by means of the following example.

Example 4.12 Consider the data dependency

$$r : \; E(x, z) \rightarrow \exists y \, E(x, y)$$

and the database $D = \{E(a, b)\}$. Under the standard chase, the dependency is satisfied and the chase terminates without any application of a chase step. Under the oblivious skolem chase only a tuple $E(a, n_1)$ is added, whereas under the oblivious naive chase an infinite number of tuples $E(a, n_1), E(a, n_2), E(a, n_3), \ldots$ is added. Consider now the set of TGDs

$$r_1 : \; E(x, z) \rightarrow \exists y \, E(x, y)$$
$$r_2 : \; E(x, z) \rightarrow E(z, x)$$

and the above database D. In this case, under standard chase only the tuple $E(b, a)$ is added to D, whereas under both versions of the oblivious skolem chase an infinite number of tuples is added. □

Let Σ be a set of dependencies. We denote with Σ_n the set of dependencies derived from Σ by replacing every TGD $\forall\mathbf{x}\,\forall\mathbf{z}\,\phi(\mathbf{x}, \mathbf{z}) \rightarrow \exists\mathbf{y}\,\psi(\mathbf{x}, \mathbf{y})$ with $\forall\mathbf{x}\,\forall\mathbf{z}\,(\phi(\mathbf{x}, \mathbf{z}) \rightarrow \exists\mathbf{y}\,\psi(\mathbf{x}, \mathbf{y}))$, that is by interpreting existentially quantified variables within the scope of all universally quantified variables. $ONchase(D, \Sigma)$ denotes a chase algorithm, known as *oblivious naive chase* applied to $(D, sk(\Sigma_n))$, where any time a new skolem term is derived it is immediately replaced by a new labeled null. Analogously, Σ_s the set of dependencies derived from Σ by replacing every TGD $\forall\mathbf{x}\,\forall\mathbf{z}\,\phi(\mathbf{x}, \mathbf{z}) \rightarrow \exists\mathbf{y}\,\psi(\mathbf{x}, \mathbf{y})$ with $\forall\mathbf{x}\,(\forall\mathbf{z}\,\phi(\mathbf{x}, \mathbf{z}) \rightarrow \exists\mathbf{y}\,\psi(\mathbf{x}, \mathbf{y}))$, that is by interpreting existentially quantified variables within the scope of universally quantified variables appearing in both body and head. $OSchase(D, \Sigma)$ denotes a chase algorithm, known as *oblivious skolem chase* applied to $(D, sk(\Sigma_s))$, where any time a new skolem term is derived, it is immediately replaced by a new labeled null.

As shown in the next example, the dependency skolemization proposed in the $OSchase$ algorithm implements a more refined way to manage the new null values inserted in the database by the chase, with respect to the *ingenuous* management of the $ONchase$ algorithm, which can easily produce non-terminating sequences.

Example 4.13 Consider again the database $D = \{E(a, b)\}$ and the data dependency $r : E(x, z) \rightarrow \exists y\, E(x, y)$ of Example 4.12. The skolemized dependency derived from r is

$$r' : E(x, z) \rightarrow E(x, f_y^r(x, z)) .$$

The application of the $ONchase$ algorithm produces the tuples $E(a, f_y^r(a, b))$ which is replaced by $E(a, \eta_1)$, $E(a, f_y^r(a, \eta_1))$ which is replaced by $E(a, \eta_2)$, $E(a, f_y^r(a, \eta_2))$ which is replaced by $E(a, \eta_3)$, and so on.

Considering the oblivious skolem chase, the skolemized dependency derived from r is

$$r' : E(x, z) \rightarrow E(x, f_y^r(x)) .$$

The application of the $OSchase$ algorithm produces only one tuple $E(a, f_y^r(a))$ which is replaced by $E(a, \eta_1)$. □

The oblivious chase here discussed captures the original definitions proposed by Meier et al. [2009a] and Marnette [2009], although in the original proposal of the oblivious skolem chase EGDs were not taken into account. The motivations was that the semantics of the oblivious skolem chase is given by the least fixed-point of the positive logic program $\mathcal{P}(\Sigma)$ (the logic program obtained from Σ) computed over the database D, and EGDs are not monotone. However, the original version of the oblivious skolem chase can be extended to also deal with EGDs by replacing them with "equivalent" TGDs [Gottlob and Nash, 2008, Marnette, 2009]. In order to distinguish oblivious naive chase steps from standard chase steps, arrows denoting mappings are also labeled with an asterisk. Therefore, in the $ONchase$ algorithm, if the result of applying a dependency r to K with h is K', we will write $K \overset{*,r,h}{\to} K'$.

In the following, two important properties for the oblivious (naive or skolem) chase are explicit. The first one relies on the fact that there always exists a homomorphism from the oblivious (naive or skolem) chase to the standard chase. As a consequence, the oblivious chase also produces a universal solution and can be used in lieu of the standard one.

Proposition 4.14 [Cali et al., 2008] *Consider a database D and a set Σ of TGDs and EGDs over the same database schema. Then there exists a homomorphism h such that $h(ONchase(\Sigma, D)) \subseteq chase(\Sigma, D)$.* $\square$

Proposition 4.15 *Consider a database D and a set Σ of TGDs over the same database schema. Then there exists a homomorphism h such that $h(OSchase(\Sigma, D)) \subseteq chase(\Sigma, D)$.* $\square$

The second property regards the fact that the universal solution produced by the oblivious (naive or skolem) chase is unique.

Proposition 4.16 *If the (naive or skolem) oblivious chase terminates with database input D and set of dependencies input Σ, then the instances returned by any non-deterministic execution of the algorithm are isomorphically equivalent.* $\square$

4.6 CORE CHASE

Deutsch et al. [2008] showed that, even if the result of a chase sequence is a universal solution, the chase is not a complete algorithm for finding universal solutions. In fact, we have that, whenever several alternative chase steps could be applied, the chase picks one non-deterministically so that in some cases there is not a unique canonical universal solution, whereas in other cases there is no finite chase. Thus, there are instances and sets of data dependencies for which certain choices lead to terminating chase sequences, while others to non-termination. Moreover, in some cases, we cannot produce a universal solution by the chase, as all chase sequences are non-terminating, although a finite solution does exist.

Example 4.17 [Deutsch et al., 2008] Consider the following set $\Sigma_{4.17}$ of TGDs:

$$
\begin{aligned}
r_0: &&& \to & E(u, v) \wedge E(v, u) \\
r_1: & E(x, y) \wedge E(y, x) & \to & E(u, u) \\
r_2: && E(x, y) & \to & E(x, u) \wedge E(u, y)
\end{aligned}
$$

The instance $\{E(\eta_i, \eta_i)\}$ is a universal model, yet it is easy to see that any chase sequence starting with $D = \{\}$ must be infinite. $\square$

In order to identify a universal solution whenever it exists, a variant of the chase, called *core chase*, has been introduced [Deutsch et al., 2008]. Informally speaking, each step in the core chase consists of two sub-steps: (a) do one step of the *parallel chase*, i.e., fire all constraints that apply; and (b) compute the core of the result.

Definition 4.18   (Core chase step)   [Deutsch et al., 2008] Let Σ be a set of data dependencies and let I, J, K be three database instances defined over the same database schema. We say that I is derived from K through a *parallel chase step* and write $K \overset{\Sigma}{\Rightarrow} I$ if i) $K \not\models \Sigma$ and ii) $I = \bigcup_{r \in \Sigma, K \overset{r,h}{\Rightarrow} K'} K'$. Moreover, we say that J is derived from K through a *core chase step* and write $K \overset{\Sigma}{\Rightarrow} J$ if $K \overset{\Sigma}{\Rightarrow} I$ and $J = core(I)$ (cf. Sec. 4.2). □

The definition of core chase sequence derives from the chase sequence by using a core chase step instead of a chase step. Observe that core chase sequences are determined up to isomorphism as well.

Example 4.19   Consider again the set of data dependencies $\Sigma_{4.17}$ of Example 4.17 and the database instance $D = \{\}$. At the first step, only the TGD r_0 can be applied by producing the instance $D_1' = \{E(\eta_1, \eta_2), E(\eta_2, \eta_1)\}$. Then, the core of D_1' is computed, resulting in $D_1 = core(D_1') = \{E(\eta_1, \eta_2), E(\eta_2, \eta_1)\}$. At the next step, rules r_1 and r_2 with all possible homomorphisms are applied producing a database $D_2' = \{E(\eta_1, \eta_2), E(\eta_2, \eta_1), E(\eta_3, \eta_3), E(\eta_1, \eta_4), E(\eta_4, \eta_1), E(\eta_2, \eta_5), E(\eta_5, \eta_2)\}$. The core of D_2' gives the database $D_2 = core(D_2') = \{E(\eta_3, \eta_3)\}$. At this point we have that $D_2 \models \Sigma_{4.17}$, and the core chase produced a universal solution. □

It has been shown that if D is a database instance and Σ is a set of TGDs and EGDs, then there exists a universal solution for Σ and D if and only if the core chase of D with Σ terminates and yields such a solution, that is, the core chase is complete for finding universal solutions. The universal solution produced by the core chase is called *core universal solution*.

4.7   COMPARISON AMONG CHASE ALGORITHMS

Termination conditions for all chase sequences (resp. for at least one chase sequence) under standard (SC), naive oblivious (NOC), skolem oblivious (NOC), and core chase (CC) will be denoted by $TOC_\forall[SC]$, $TOC_\forall[NOC]$, $TOC_\forall[SOC]^2$, and $TOC_\forall[CC]$ (resp. $TOC_\exists[SC]$, $TOC_\exists[NOC]$, $TOC_\exists[SOC]$ and $TOC_\exists[CC]$).

Definition 4.20   A set of data dependencies Σ is in $TOC_\forall[C]$ for $C \in \{SC, NOC, SOC, CC\}$ if, for every database instance D, all the C-chase sequences of D with Σ are finite.

A set of data dependencies Σ is in $TOC_\exists[C]$ for $C \in \{SC, NOC, SOC, CC\}$ if, for every database instance D, at least one C-chase sequence of D with Σ is finite.

---

[2]This class has already been defined by Marnette [2009] under the name of TOC.

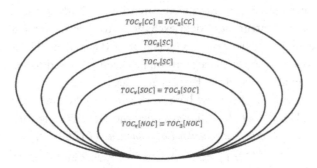

Figure 4.1: Comparison among the termination conditions for chase algorithms.

Proposition 4.21   [Deutsch et al., 2008, Marnette, 2009, Onet, 2012] *It is undecidable if* $\Sigma \in$ $TOC_\forall[C]$ *or* $\Sigma \in TOC_\exists[C]$ *for* $C \in \{SC, NOC, SOC, CC\}$. $\square$

From the discussions made in the previous sections it easy to see that, in general, $TOC_\forall[C] \subsetneq$ $TOC_\exists[C]$ as the termination for all sequences implies the termination of at least one sequence. Moreover, we have that $TOC_\forall[C] \equiv TOC_\exists[C]$, for $C \in \{NOC, SOC, CC\}$ as, in the case of core chase, all chase steps are applied in parallel, while in the case of the oblivious (naive or skolem) chase the solution produced is unique.

Theorem 4.22   [Deutsch et al., 2008, Onet, 2012]

1. $TOC_\forall[SC] \subsetneq TOC_\exists[SC] \subsetneq TOC_\forall[CC] \equiv TOC_\exists[CC]$.

2. $TOC_\forall[NOC] \equiv TOC_\exists[NOC] \subsetneq TOC_\forall[SOC] \equiv TOC_\exists[SOC] \subsetneq TOC_\forall[SC]$. $\square$

In conclusion, for all the chase variation algorithms presented in this chapter, in case they terminate for a given input, the instance returned is a solution for the input instance and the input set of dependencies. Consequently, for all the chase algorithms, in case they terminate for a given input, the instances returned from each of these algorithms are homomorphically equivalent. Figure 4.1 presents a comparison among the termination conditions for all chase algorithms.

BIBLIOGRAPHIC NOTES

The chase is a fixpoint algorithm proposed more than 30 years ago by Aho et al. [1979a] and Maier et al. [1979] for testing both tableau queries and logical implications in presence of functional dependencies and join dependencies (see Chapter 6). Other related results and preliminaries ideas can be found in Aho et al. [1979a,b], Maier et al. [1981], Vardi [1983]. Beeri and Vardi [1984] extended the chase technique to the more general embedded dependencies.

The chase has received an increasing attention, in both database theory and practical applications, such as data integration, data exchange, etc. (see Chapter 8). In the context of query optimization of conjunctive queries in presence of TGDs and EGDs, a variant of the chase algorithm, called the *chase and backchase* algorithm, has been proposed to solve the query minimization problem [Deutsch et al., 1999, 2006, Popa et al., 2000].

The chase algorithms discussed here work with specific kinds of data dependencies, namely TGDs and EGDs. Deutsch et al. [2008] extended the core chase algorithm in order to deal with the more general *negation disjunctive embedded dependencies* ($TGD^{\vee,\neg}$), i.e., dependencies of the form $\exists \mathbf{w} \, (\bigvee_{1 \leq i \leq n} \phi_i(\mathbf{x}, \mathbf{y})) \rightarrow \exists \mathbf{z} \, (\bigvee_{1 \leq i \leq m} \psi_i(\mathbf{x}, \mathbf{z}))$, where each ϕ_i and ψ_i is a conjunction of relational atoms, negated relational atoms, equations, or inequalities.

Chasing *disjunctive embedded dependencies* $TGD^{\vee}$, i.e., $TGD^{\vee,\neg}$ with no negated atoms, was also investigated by Marnette and Geerts [2010], while chasing TGDs with inequalities was investigated by Karvounarakis and Tannen [2008].

Hernich and Schweikardt [2007] introduced, in the context of data exchange, a new chase-based algorithm, called the α-*chase*, to compute the CWA-presolutions, useful for computing the CWA-solution set [Libkin, 2006].

CHAPTER 5

Chase Termination

This chapter presents an overview of the well-known chase termination conditions. They guarantee for every database D the termination of all chase sequences.

As discussed in the previous chapter, the execution of the chase algorithm involves the insertion of tuples with possible null values, and the changing of nulls, which can be made equal to constants or other null values. However, the insertion of tuples with new (null) values could result in a non-terminating execution. The following example shows a case where a given database does not satisfy a set of data dependencies (also called constraints), and the application of the chase algorithm produces a new consistent database by adding tuples with nulls.

Example 5.1   Consider the set of constraints $\Sigma_{5.1}$:

$$\forall x \ N(x) \rightarrow \exists y \ E(x, y)$$
$$\forall x \forall y \ S(x) \wedge E(x, y) \rightarrow N(y) \quad '$$

where the relations N and S store normal nodes and special nodes, respectively, whereas E stores edges. The second constraint states that if there exists an edge from x to y and x is a special node, then y must also be a (normal) node. The first constraint states that every normal node must have an outgoing edge.

Assume that the database contains the tuples $S(a)$, $E(b, a)$. Since the second constraint is not satisfied, the tuple $N(a)$ is inserted. This update operation fires the first constraint to insert the tuple $E(a, n_1)$, where n_1 is a new labeled null. At this point the chase terminates since the database is consistent, i.e., the second constraint cannot be fired because n_1 is not in the relation S. The output database is consistent as both dependencies are satisfied.   □

However, it is important to observe that if we delete atom $S(x)$ from the second constraint, the chase will never terminate, as an infinite number of tuples will be added to the database.

The problem recently investigated, known as *chase termination*, consists of the identification of sufficient conditions, based on structural properties of the input set of constraints that guarantee that the chase fixpoint terminates independently from the database instance.

In the following, we will denote by $\mathcal{C}$ the class of sets of constraints satisfying a given criterion C.

5.1   CHASE TERMINATION CRITERIA

The chase termination criteria presented in this section have been designed to guarantee the termination of the standard chase, except for the super-weak acyclicity, defined for the oblivious skolem chase (cf. Section 4.5).

However, in order to relate termination of the standard and of the (naive) oblivious chase, a dependency transformation, known as *enrichment of dependencies*, has been proposed [Grahne and Onet, 2011]. More specifically, let Σ be a set of dependencies over a schema $\mathbf{R}$, the enrichment of Σ, denoted as $\hat{\Sigma}$, consists in converting each TGD $r : \phi(\mathbf{x}, \mathbf{y}) \to \exists \mathbf{z} \ \psi(\mathbf{x}, \mathbf{z})$ into the TGD $\hat{r} : \phi(\mathbf{x}, \mathbf{y}) \to \exists \mathbf{z} \ \psi(\mathbf{x}, \mathbf{z}), H(\mathbf{x}, \mathbf{y})$, where H is a new relational symbol that does not appear in $\mathbf{R}$. Then, the enrichment of Σ is $\hat{\Sigma} = \{\hat{r} : r \in \Sigma\}$.

Theorem 5.2   [Grahne and Onet, 2011] $ONchase(\Sigma, K)$ *terminates if and only if* $chase(\hat{\Sigma}, K)$ *terminates.*   □

Moreover, it is easy to see that, to relate termination of the standard and skolem oblivious chase, we have to add $H(\mathbf{x})$ instead of $H(\mathbf{x}, \mathbf{y})$ to each TGD. Observe that the database K used in $ONchase(\Sigma, K)$ and $chase(\hat{\Sigma}, K)$ is the same, but the resulting databases, obtained from the application of the two chase algorithms, may be different.

Weak Acyclicity

The first and basic criterion concerning the identification of sufficient conditions, determined by the structure of TGDs, guaranteeing chase termination, is known as *weak acyclicity* (WA) [Deutsch and Tannen, 2003, Fagin et al., 2005a] inspired by Hull and Yoshikawa [1990]. The criterion is based on the structural properties of a graph $dep(\Sigma)$, known as *dependency graph*, derived from the input set of TGDs Σ.

Let Σ be a set of TGDs over a database schema $\mathbf{R}$, then $pos(\Sigma)$ denotes the set of positions R_i such that R denotes a relational predicate of $\mathbf{R}$ and there is an R-atom appearing in Σ.

Definition 5.3   (Weakly acyclic set of TGDs)   Let Σ be a set of TGDs over a fixed schema. Construct a directed graph $dep(\Sigma) = (pos(\Sigma), E)$, known as *dependency graph*, whose nodes correspond to the positions in $pos(\Sigma)$ and set E of edges is obtained as follows: for every TGD $\phi(\mathbf{x}, \mathbf{z}) \to \exists \mathbf{y} \psi(\mathbf{x}, \mathbf{y})$ in Σ and for every x in $\mathbf{x}$ that occurs in ϕ in position R_i:

1. for every occurrence of x in ψ in position S_j, add an edge $R_i \to S_j$ (if it does not already exist);

2. for every existentially quantified variable y and for every occurrence of y in ψ in position T_k, add a special edge $R_i \xrightarrow{\ast} T_k$ (if it does not already exist).

Then, Σ is *weakly acyclic* if the corresponding dependency graph $dep(\Sigma)$ has no cycle going through a special edge.   □

Example 5.4   Consider the below set of constraints $\Sigma_{5.4}$:

$$r_1 :\ N(x) \to \exists y\ E(x, y)$$
$$r_2 :\ S(y) \wedge E(x, y) \to N(y)$$

derived from the set $\Sigma_{5.1}$ of Example 5.1 by replacing the atom $S(x)$ with $S(y)$ in the body of r_2. The dependency graph $dep(\Sigma_{5.4})$ contains the following arcs: $N_1 \to E_1$, $N_1 \overset{*}{\to} E_2$, $E_2 \to N_1$ and $S_1 \to N_1$. Since $dep(\Sigma_{5.4})$ contains a cycle with a special edge $(N_1 \overset{*}{\to} E_2 \to N_1)$, $\Sigma_{5.4}$ is not weakly acyclic.   □

The weak acyclicity criterion guarantees, for all database instances, that all chase sequences terminate. Clearly, the problem of checking whether a set of TGDs is weakly acyclic is polynomial in the size of Σ. Fagin et al. [2005a] showed that if Σ is the union of a weakly acyclic set of TGDs with a set of EGDs, and D is a database instance, then there exists a polynomial in the size of D that bounds the length of every chase sequence of D with Σ.

A slight restriction of weak acyclicity has been defined by Hernich and Schweikardt [2007] by adding special edges in the dependency graph. More specifically, $dep(\Sigma)$ is extended by adding a special edge from position R_i and T_k whenever there is a TGD $\phi(\mathbf{x}, \mathbf{z}) \to \exists \mathbf{y} \psi (\mathbf{x}, \mathbf{y}) \in \Sigma$ such that a variable $z \in \mathbf{z}$ appears in R_i and an existentially quantified variable $y \in \mathbf{y}$ appears in T_k. The new graph is called *extended dependency graph*. A set of dependencies Σ is said to be *richly acyclic* if the extended dependency graph of Σ has no cycle going through a special edge. The following lemma is immediate.

Lemma 5.5   [Grahne and Onet, 2011] *Let Σ be a richly acyclic set of dependencies. Then $\hat{\Sigma}$ is weakly acyclic.*   □

It follows that the rich acyclicity criterion guarantees, for all database instances, the termination of the naive oblivious chase in PTIME.

Stratification

The first extension of weak acyclicity is the stratification criterion (Str), proposed by Deutsch et al. [2008]. The idea behind stratification is to decompose the set of constraints into independent subsets, where each subset consists of constraints that may fire each other, and to check each component separately for weak acyclicity.

Definition 5.6   (Precedence relation)   [Deutsch et al., 2008] Given a set of constraints Σ and two constraints $r_1, r_2 \in \Sigma$, we say that $r_1 \prec r_2$ iff there exists a relational database instance K and two homomorphisms h_1 and h_2 such that:

i) $K \stackrel{r_1, h_1}{\Rightarrow} J$,

ii) $J \not\models h_2(r_2)$, and

iii) $K \models h_2(r_2)$. □

Intuitively, $r_1 \prec r_2$ means that firing r_1 can cause the firing of r_2.

Definition 5.7   (Stratified constraints)   [Deutsch et al., 2008] The *chase graph* $G(\Sigma) = (\Sigma, E)$ of a set of constraints Σ contains a directed edge (r_1, r_2) between two constraints iff $r_1 \prec r_2$. We say that Σ is *stratified* iff the constraints in every cycle of $G(\Sigma)$ are weakly acyclic. □

Example 5.8   Consider the set of dependencies $\Sigma_{5.4}$ from Example 5.4. The chase graph $G(\Sigma_{5.4})$ contains the unique edge $r_2 \rightarrow r_1$. Indeed:

- $r_2 \prec r_1$, as for $K = \{E(a, b), S(b)\}$, $h_1 = \{x/a, y/b\}$ and $h_2 = \{x/b\}$, we have that i) $K \not\models h_1(r_2)$ and the application of r_1 with h produces $J = D \cup n(b)$, and ii) $J \not\models h_2(r_1)$ (while $K \models h_2(r_1)$) — that is the firing of r_2, using the database K, caused the next firing of r_1;

- $r_1 \not\prec r_2$, as if we take a database K' and an homomorphism h_1' such that $K' \not\models h_1'(r_1)$ (e.g., $K' = \{N(a)\}$ and $h_1' = \{x/a\}$), the firing of r_2 produces a new database J' (e.g., $J' = \{N(a), E(a, \eta_1)\}$) which cannot fire r_2 as the null value introduced in position E_2 cannot be contained in relation S.

Obviously, $r_1 \not\prec r_1$ and $r_2 \not\prec r_2$ as in both dependencies there are no two unifying atoms A and B, in the head and body, respectively. Consequently, being $G(\Sigma_{5.4})$ acyclic, $\Sigma_{5.4}$ is stratified. □

Example 5.9   [Deutsch et al., 2008] Consider the set $\Sigma_{5.9}$ consisting of the constraint

$$r : E(x, y) \wedge E(y, x) \rightarrow \exists z \, \exists w \, E(y, z) \wedge E(z, w) \wedge E(w, x)$$

stating that each node involved in a cycle of length 2 is also involved in a cycle of length 4 and the two cycles share an edge. Dependency r cannot fire itself, that is $r \not\prec r$, as if we take a generic database $K = \{E(a, b), E(b, a)\}$, the application of r produces a new database $J = K \cup \{E(b, \eta_1), E(\eta_1, \eta_2), E(\eta_2, a)\}$ which satisfies r. Since $G(\Sigma_{5.9})$ is acyclic, $\Sigma_{5.9}$ is stratified. □

Deutsch et al. [2008] showed that the problem of deciding whether a set of constraints is stratified is in $co\mathcal{NP}$ and that stratification strictly generalizes the weak acyclicity criterion ($\mathcal{WA} \subsetneq \mathcal{S}tr$).

C-stratification   Stratification guarantees, as shown by Meier et al. [2009b], that, for every database D, there is a chase sequence which terminates in polynomial time in the size of D, i.e., $Str \subsetneq TOC_\exists[SC]$, but does not guarantee that all chase sequences terminates. The following example shows such a case.

Example 5.10   Consider the following set of constraints $\Sigma_{5.10}$:

$$r_1 : N(x) \rightarrow \exists y \, E(x, y)$$
$$r_2 : N(x) \rightarrow E(x, x)$$
$$r_3 : E(x, y) \wedge E(x, x) \rightarrow N(x) \,.$$

$\Sigma_{5.10}$ is stratified since $r_3 \prec r_1$, $r_3 \prec r_2 \prec r_3$ (but $r_1 \not\prec r_3$), and the set of constraints $\{r_2, r_3\}$ is weakly acyclic. Moreover, assuming that the database only contains the tuple $R(a)$, the chase firing repeatedly r_1, r_2 and r_3 never terminates ($R(a)$, $E(a, \eta_1)$, $E(a, a)$, $R(\eta_1)$, ...), while the chase which never fires r_1 terminates successfully.   □

In order to cope with this problem, a variation of stratification, called *c-stratification* criterion ($CStr$), was proposed by Meier et al. [2009b]. Basically, c-stratification defines a different chase graph and applies a constraint whenever its body is satisfied (i.e., it uses the oblivious naive chase).

Definition 5.11   (C-Stratified constraints)   Given two constraints $r_1, r_2 \in \Sigma$, we say that $r_1 \prec_c r_2$ iff there exists a relational database instance K and two homomorphisms h_1 and h_2 such that:

i) $K \overset{*,r_1,h_1}{\rightarrow} J$,

ii) $J \not\models h_2(r_2)$, and

iii) $K \models h_2(r_2)$.

The *c-chase graph* $G_c(\Sigma) = (\Sigma, E)$ of a set of constraints Σ contains a directed edge (r_1, r_2) between two constraints iff $r_1 \prec_c r_2$. We say that Σ is c-stratified iff the constraints in every cycle of $G_c(\Sigma)$ are weakly acyclic.   □

Since c-stratification guarantees the termination of all chase sequences (in contrast to stratification), the class of c-stratified constraints is strictly included in the set of stratified ones ($CStr \subsetneq Str$). Considering the two previous examples we have that the set of constraints $\Sigma_{5.10}$ in Example 5.10 is stratified, but not c-stratified, whereas the set of Constraints $\Sigma_{5.9}$ of Example 5.9 is c-stratified.

The problem of checking whether a set of constraints is c-stratified is in $co\mathcal{NP}$ (as the case of stratification). As well as weak acyclicity, c-stratification guarantees that for every database D there exists a polynomial in the size of D that bounds the length of every chase sequence of D with Σ [Meier et al., 2009b].

Safety

A different extension of weak acyclicity, called *safety* criterion (SC), which takes into account only affected positions has been proposed [Meier et al., 2009a]. An affected position denotes a position which could be associated with null values, that is it can also take values from *Nulls*.

Definition 5.12 (Affected positions) [Cali et al., 2008] Let Σ be a set TGDs. The set of *affected positions aff(Σ)* of Σ is defined as follows. Let R_i be a position occurring in the head of some TGD $r \in \Sigma$, then:

- if an existentially quantified variable appears in R_i, then $R_i \in aff(\Sigma)$;

- if the same universally quantified variable x appears both in position R_i and only in affected positions in the body of r, then $R_i \in aff(\Sigma)$. $\qquad\square$

Example 5.13 Consider the following set of constraints $\Sigma_{5.13}$:

$$r_1 : \forall x \ N(x) \rightarrow \exists y \ E(x, y)$$
$$r_2 : \forall x \ \forall y \ E(x, y) \rightarrow N(y).$$

We have that position E_2 is affected as contains the existentially quantified variable y. Moreover, position also N_1 is affected as the variable x in r_2 appears in the body of r_2 only in affected positions. Consequently, position E_1 also is affected.

Considering the set of constraints of Example 5.4, which can be derived from the above ones by adding the atom $S(y)$ in the body of dependency r_2. Position E_2 is affected as contains the existentially quantified variable y. Moreover, position N_1 is not affected as variable y in dependency r_2 does not appear only in affected positions. Consequently, also position E_1 is not affected. $\qquad\square$

Definition 5.14 (Safe set of TGDs) [Meier et al., 2009a] Let Σ be a set of TGDs, then $prop(\Sigma) = (aff(\Sigma), E)$ denotes the *propagation graph* of Σ defined as follows. For every TGD $\phi(\mathbf{x}, \mathbf{z}) \rightarrow \exists \mathbf{y} \ \psi(\mathbf{x}, \mathbf{y})$ and for every x in $\mathbf{x}$ occurring in ϕ in position R_i then:

- if x occurs only in affected positions in ϕ then for every occurrence of x in ψ in position S_j there is an edge $R_i \rightarrow S_j$ in E;

- if x occurs only in affected positions in ϕ then, for every y in $\mathbf{y}$ and for every occurrence of y in ψ in position S_j there is a special edge $R_i \overset{*}{\rightarrow} S_j$ in E.

A set of constraints Σ is said to be *safe* if the corresponding propagation graph $prop(\Sigma)$ has no cycles going through a special edge. □

Consider again the set $\Sigma_{5.4}$ from Example $\Sigma_{5.4}$. It is safe since the unique affected position is E_2 and the propagation graph $prop(\Sigma_{5.4})$ does not have any edge. Remember that $\Sigma_{5.4}$ is stratified but not weakly acyclic.

On the other hand, the stratified set $\Sigma_{5.9}$ is not safe as all positions are affected and the associated propagation graph contains cycles with special edges. The following example presents a safe set of constraints which is not stratified.

Example 5.15   Let $\Sigma_{5.15}$ be the set of below constraints:

$$r_1 : S(x) \wedge E(x, y) \wedge E(y, z) \rightarrow \exists w\ E(w, x)$$
$$r_2 : E(x, y) \wedge E(y, z) \rightarrow S(z)$$

stating that each special node having an outgoing path of length 2 has an incoming edge (r_1) and that each path of length 2 ends in a special node (r_2). Since $\mathit{aff}(\Sigma_{5.15}) = \{E_1\}$ the propagation graph does not contain any edge and, therefore, $\Sigma_{5.15}$ is safe. Observe that $\Sigma_{5.15}$ is not stratified since $r_1 \prec r_2, r_2 \prec r_1$, and the dependency graph of $\{r_1, r_2\}$ contains cycles with special edges. □

Clearly, the safety criterion strictly generalizes the weak acyclicity criterion ($\mathcal{WA} \subsetneq \mathcal{SC}$), it is not comparable with (c-)stratification (see examples 5.9 and 5.15), and the problem of checking whether a set of TGDs is safe is polynomial in the size of $|\Sigma|$. Moreover, for every Σ being the union of a safe set of TGDs with a set of EGDs, and for every database instance D, there exists a polynomial in the size of D that bounds the length of every chase sequence of D with Σ.

Safe Restriction

A more refined extension of both c-stratification and safety criteria has been proposed under the name of *safe restriction* (SR) criterion [Meier et al., 2009a,b]. Basically, safe restriction refines stratification by considering constraint firing and possible propagation of null values together.

In order to introduce this concept we need some further definitions. For any set of positions P and a TGD r, $aff(r, P)$ denotes the set of positions π from the head of r such that (i) for every universally quantified variable x in π, x occurs in the body of r only in positions from P or (ii) π contains an existentially quantified variable.

For any $r_1, r_2 \in \Sigma$ and $P \subseteq pos(\Sigma), r_1 \prec_P r_2$ if:

1. $r_1 \prec_c r_2$ (i.e., there exists a database instance K and two homomorphisms h_1 and h_2 such that i) $K \overset{r_1, h_1}{\rightarrow} J$, ii) $J \not\models h_2(r_2)$ and iii) $K \models h_2(r_2)$); and

2. there is null value propagated from the body to the head of $h_2(r_2)$ such that it occurs in K only in positions from P.

Definition 5.16   (Safe restriction)   [Meier et al., 2009a,b] A 2-restriction system is a pair $(G'(\Sigma), P)$, where $G'(\Sigma) = (\Sigma, E)$ is a directed graph and $P \subseteq pos(\Sigma)$ such that:

1. for all $(r_1, r_2) \in E$: if r_1 is TGD, then $\mathit{aff}(r_1, P) \cap pos(\Sigma) \subseteq P$, whereas if r_2 is TGD, then $\mathit{aff}(r_2, P) \cap pos(\Sigma) \subseteq P$, and

2. $r_1 \prec_P r_2 \Rightarrow (r_1, r_2) \in E$.

Σ is called *safely restricted* if and only if there is a restriction system $(G'(\Sigma), P)$ for Σ such that every strongly connected component in $G'(\Sigma)$ is safe.   □

A 2-restriction system is *minimal* if it is obtained from $((\Sigma, \emptyset), \emptyset)$ by a repeated application of conditions 1 and 2 of Definition 5.16 (until both conditions hold considering all constraints) such that, in case Condition 1 is applied, P is extended only by those positions that are required to satisfy the condition. Meier [2010] showed that Σ is safely restricted if and only if every strongly connected component in $G'(\Sigma)$ is safe, where $(G'(\Sigma), P)$ is the minimal 2-restriction system for Σ.

Example 5.17   [Meier et al., 2009a] Consider the below set of constraints $\Sigma_{5.17}$:

$$r_1 : S(x) \wedge E(x, y) \to E(y, x)$$
$$r_2 : S(x) \wedge E(x, y) \to \exists z \, E(y, z) \wedge E(z, x)$$

asserting that each special node with an outgoing edge has cycles of length 2 and 3, respectively. As position S_1 is not affected, the insertion of nulls in position E_1 does not contribute to introduce further tuples with null values. Assuming $P = \{E_1, E_2\}$ we have that $r_1 \not\prec_P r_1, r_1 \not\prec_P r_2, r_2 \prec_P r_1$ and $r_2 \not\prec_P r_2$. Thus, $G'(\Sigma_{5.17}) = (\{r_1, r_2\}, \{(r_2, r_1)\})$ and, consequently, $\Sigma_{5.17}$ is safely restricted.
□

It is worth noting that $\Sigma_{5.17}$ is neither safe (since the propagation graph $prop(\Sigma_{5.17})$ has a cycle $E_2 \xrightarrow{*} E_2$) nor c-stratified (since the chase graph $G_c(\Sigma_{5.17})$ has a cycle $r_1 \prec_c r_2 \prec_c r_1$).

Inductive Restriction

Safely restriction has been extended into a criterion called *inductive restriction* (*IR*), whose main idea is to decompose a given constraint set into smaller subsets (in a more refined way than safe restriction). In particular, *IR* first computes the system $(G'(\Sigma), P)$ and partitions Σ into $\Sigma_1, ..., \Sigma_n$, where each Σ_i is a set of constraints defining a strongly connected component in $G'(\Sigma)$, next, if $n = 1$ the safety criterion is applied to Σ, otherwise the *IR* criterion is applied inductively to each Σ_i.

Example 5.18   Assume we add to $\Sigma_{5.17}$ the constraint $r_3: \to \exists x \exists y \, S(x) \wedge E(x, y)$. The new set of constraints, denoted as $\Sigma_{5.18}$, is not safely restricted, but is inductively restricted since by partitioning $\Sigma_{5.18}$ into strongly connected components we obtain the two components $\{r_3\}$ and $\{r_1, r_2\}$ which are both safely restricted.   □

The problem of checking whether a set of constraints is inductively restricted is in $co\mathcal{NP}$. As well as c-stratification and safety, inductive restriction guarantees that for every database D there exists a polynomial in the size of D that bounds the length of every chase sequence of D with Σ [Meier et al., 2009b]. In that work it has been also shown that $\mathcal{CStr} \subsetneq \mathcal{SR} \subsetneq \mathcal{IR}$ and $\mathcal{SC} \subsetneq \mathcal{SR}$.

Inductive restriction has been further extended by considering not only the relationships among pairs of constraints, but general sequences of m constraints, with $m \geq 2$ [Meier et al., 2009a]. The use of sequences of $m \geq 2$ constraints allows a hierarchy of classes where each class is characterized by m and denoted by $\mathcal{T}[m]$, with $\mathcal{T}[2] = \mathcal{IR}$ and $\mathcal{T}[m] \subsetneq \mathcal{T}[m+1]$.

Example 5.19   The set of constraints $\Sigma_{5.19}^n$ consisting of the TGD

$$S(x) \wedge E(x, y_1, ..., y_n) \rightarrow E(x, y_1, ..., y_n, z)$$

belongs to $\mathcal{T}[n+1] - \mathcal{T}[n]$.   □

In the following we do not further discuss the $\mathcal{T}$-hierarchy as: (i) the complexity of checking whether a set of constraints is in $\mathcal{T}[m]$ increases, with respect to $\mathcal{IR}$, with a factor $|\Sigma|^m$; (ii) we do not have any criterion to fix m; and (iii) the same extension can be also defined for other stratification-based criteria such as the ones presented next (WA-stratification and local stratification).

Super-weak Acyclicity

Super-weak acyclicity (SwA) [Marnette, 2009] builds a *trigger graph* $\Upsilon(\Sigma) = (\Sigma, E)$ where edges define relations among constraints. An edge $r_i \rightsquigarrow r_j$ means that a null value introduced by a constraint r_i is propagated (directly or indirectly) into the head of r_j.

Let Σ be a set of TGDs and let $\mathcal{LP}(\Sigma)$ be the logic program obtained from $sk(\Sigma_s)$ by deleting quantification. As stated in Sections 4.3 and 4.5, Σ_s is the set of dependencies derived from Σ by replacing every TGD $\forall\mathbf{x}\,\forall\mathbf{z}\,\phi(\mathbf{x}, \mathbf{z}) \rightarrow \exists\mathbf{y}\,\psi(\mathbf{x}, \mathbf{y})$ with $\forall\mathbf{x}\,(\forall\mathbf{z}\,\phi(\mathbf{x}, \mathbf{z}) \rightarrow \exists\mathbf{y}\,\psi(\mathbf{x}, \mathbf{y}))$, that is by interpreting existentially quantified variables within the scope of universally quantified variables appearing in both body and head.

A *place* is a pair (a, i) where a is an atom of $\mathcal{LP}(\Sigma)$ and $0 \leq i \leq ar(a)$. Given a TGD r and an existential variable y in the head of r, $Out(r, y)$ denotes the set of places (called *output places*) in the head of $\mathcal{LP}(r)$ where a term of the form $f_y^r(\mathbf{x})$ occurs. Let r be a TGD r and let x be a universal variable of r, $In(r, x)$ denotes the set of places (called *input places*) in the body of r where x occurs.

Example 5.20   Consider the set of TGDs $\Sigma_{5.20}$:

$$r_1 : N(x) \rightarrow \exists y \exists z\, E(x, y, z)$$
$$r_2 : E(x, y, y) \rightarrow N(y)$$

The logic program obtained by skolemizing $\Sigma_{5.20}$ is:

$$P(\Sigma_{5.20}) = \begin{cases} r'_1 : \underset{p_1}{S(x)} \rightarrow E(\underset{p_2}{x}, \underset{p_3}{f^{r_1}_y(x)}, \underset{p_4}{f^{r_1}_z(x)}) \\ r'_2 : \underset{p_5\ p_6\ p_7}{E(x, y, y)} \rightarrow \underset{p_8}{S(y)} \end{cases}$$

and $Out(r_1, y) = \{p_3\}$, $Out(r_1, z) = \{p_4\}$, $In(r_2, y) = \{p_6, p_7\}$.   □

Given a set of variables V, a substitution θ of V is a function mapping each $v \in V$ to a finite term $\theta(v)$ built upon constants and function symbols. Two places (a, i) and (a', i) are *unifiable*, denoted as $(a, i) \sim (a', i)$, iff there exist two substitutions θ and θ' of (respectively) the variables a and a' such that $\theta(a) = \theta'(a')$. Given two sets of places Q and Q', we write $Q \sqsubseteq Q'$ iff for all $q \in Q$ there exists some $q' \in Q'$ such that $q \sim q'$.

For any set Q of places, $Move(\Sigma, Q)$ denotes the smallest set of places Q' such that $Q \subseteq Q'$, and for every constraint $r = B_r \rightarrow H_r$ in $\mathcal{LP}(\Sigma)$ and every variable x, if $\Pi_x(B_r) \sqsubseteq Q'$ then $\Pi_x(H_r) \subseteq Q'$, where $\Pi_x(B_r)$ and $\Pi_x(H_r)$ denote the sets of places in B_r and H_r where x occurs.

Definition 5.21   (Trigger graph and Super-weak Acyclicity)   [Marnette, 2009] Given a set Σ of TGDs and two TGDs $r, r' \in \Sigma$, we say that r triggers r' in Σ, and we write $r \rightsquigarrow r'$, iff there exists an existential variable y in the head of r, and a universal variable x' occurring both in the body and head of r' such that $In(r'x') \sqsubseteq Move(\Sigma, Out(r, y))$. A set of constraints Σ is super-weakly acyclic iff the trigger graph $\Upsilon(\Sigma) = (\Sigma, \{(r_1, r_2)|r_1 \rightsquigarrow r_2\})$ is acyclic.   □

Example 5.20 (cont.)   Since $Move(\Sigma_{5.20}, Out(r_1, y)) = \{p_3\}$, $Move(\Sigma_{5.20}, Out(r_1, z)) = \{p_4\}$, and $In(r_2, y)) = \{p_6, p_7\}$, we have that $In(r_2, y) \not\sqsubseteq Move(\Sigma_{5.20}, Out(r_1, y))$, and $In(r_2, y) \not\sqsubseteq Move(\Sigma_{5.20}, Out(r_1, z))$. Consequently, r_2 is not triggered by r_1 (as well as $r_1 \not\rightsquigarrow r_1$) and, therefore, $\Sigma_{5.20}$ is super-weakly acyclic.   □

Observe that the set of constraints $\Sigma_{5.20}$ is also c-stratified (the activation of r_1 cannot fire r_2 since two different nulls are introduced in positions E_2 and E_3), but it is not safe as all positions are affected and the propagation graph contains cycles with special edges.

With respect to other criteria, SwA also takes into account the fact that a variable may occur more than once in the same atom. SwA extends WA ($\mathcal{WA} \subsetneq \mathcal{SwA}$), guarantees the termination of all chase sequences in polynomial time in the size of the input database, and the problem of deciding whether a set of constraints is super-weakly acyclic is in PTIME. Moreover, it was shown in [Greco and Spezzano, 2010] that super-weak acyclicity is more general than the safety criterion ($\mathcal{SC} \subsetneq \mathcal{SwA}$).

The SwA criterion has been designed to guarantee the termination of the oblivious skolem chase, i.e., $\mathcal{SwA} \subsetneq \mathsf{TOC_V[SOC]}$. However, since $\mathsf{TOC_V[SOC]} \subsetneq \mathsf{TOC_V[SC]}$, super-weak acyclicity can be considered a sufficient condition also for the standard chase.

Local Stratification

In this section we present some improvements for termination conditions discussed in the previous section, and then we introduce the class of *locally stratified dependencies*, that generalizes all previously known classes, for which termination of the chase algorithm is guaranteed.

The idea underlying stratification, also used in its extensions (e.g., $CStr$, SR) and in the super-weak acyclicity, is to consider in the propagation of nulls how constraints may fire each other. However, there are simple cases where current criteria are not able to capture the fact that all chase sequences are finite (see, for instance, the following Example 5.24). Thus, in this section we first introduce a new version of stratification, called *WA-stratification* (*WA-Str*), which generalizes $CStr$ and guarantees, for all databases, termination of all chase sequences.

We start with some observations on the (c-)stratification definition. (C-)stratification does not specify what kind of cycles are checked (i.e., simple or general). Checking simple cycles is not correct as it may not consider all possible chase sequences. Moreover, checking general cycles means that for each strongly connected component, there is one cycle including all nodes in the component which subsumes all other cycles on the same component (in terms of constraints to be considered).

Example 5.22   Consider the following set of TGDs $\Sigma_{5.22}$:

$$
\begin{array}{rrcl}
r_1: & P(x) & \rightarrow & \exists y\ Q(x, y) \\
r_2: & Q(x, y) & \rightarrow & R(x, y) \\
r_3: & R(x, y) & \rightarrow & P(x) \\
r_4: & R(x, y) & \rightarrow & S(y, x) \\
r_5: & S(x, y) & \rightarrow & Q(x, y)
\end{array}
$$

We have that $r_1 \prec_c r_2$, $r_2 \prec_c r_3$, $r_3 \prec_c r_1$, $r_2 \prec_c r_4$, $r_4 \prec_c r_5$ and $r_5 \prec_c r_2$. The c-chase graph contains two simple cycles, $\{r_1, r_2, r_3\}$ and $\{r_2, r_4, r_5\}$, that are both weakly acyclic, and a general cycle involving all the TGDs in $\Sigma_{5.22}$ that is not weakly acyclic. $\square$

Although considering the constraints involved in every cycle is not wrong, it is equivalent to just considering the subsets of constraints involved in every strongly connected component. This is due to the fact that if the weak acyclicity property is satisfied by a set of constraints it is satisfied by all its subsets as well. Moreover, the number of cycles in a graph could be exponential, whereas the number of strongly connected components is polynomial. Thus, a first observation on (c-)stratification (in terms of correctness, if simple cycles are considered, or in terms of efficiency, if all cycles are considered) is that it refers to cycles instead of strongly connected components. A further observation is that it uses the oblivious chase for checking termination of standard chase and, as previously said, applicability of the oblivious chase is limited.

Definition 5.23   (WA-Stratification)   [Greco et al., 2011] Given a set of dependencies Σ and $r_1, r_2 \in \Sigma$, we say that $r_1 < r_2$ iff there exist a relational database instance K, homomorphisms h_1, h_2, and a set S of atoms, such that: (i) $K \not\models h_1(r_1)$; (ii) $K \overset{r_1,h_1}{\rightarrow} J$; (iii) $K \cup S \models h_2(r_2)$; (iv) $J \cup S \not\models$

$h_2(r_2)$; and (v) $Null(S) \cap (Null(J) - Null(K)) = \emptyset$ (i.e., S does not contain new null values introduced in J).

We say that Σ is *WA-stratified* (*WA-Str*) iff the constraints in every non-trivial strongly connected component of the *firing graph* $\Gamma(\Sigma) = (\Sigma, \{(r_1, r_2)|r_1 < r_2\})$ are weakly acyclic.   □

With respect to stratification, *WA-Str* also considers in the satisfaction of constraint r_2 in Definition 5.23, in addition to the database K, a set of atoms S (cond. (iii)) whose elements cannot contain null values introduced in the application of the constraint r_1 (cond. (v)). Moreover, since we are considering strongly connected components (instead of cycles), these components must not be trivial, that is they must have at least one edge, otherwise the constraint cannot be fired cyclically. As a further important observation, in the above definition we consider standard chase for both constructing the graph $\Gamma(\Sigma)$ and checking weak acyclicity.

Example 5.24   Consider the set of constraints $\Sigma_{5.24}$ consisting of the TGD

$$E(x, y) \wedge E(y, x) \rightarrow \exists z \, E(y, z) \wedge E(z, x) \,.$$

It is easy to see that, by considering standard chase, an initial database instance for which the constraint can fire itself does not exist, while, by considering the oblivious chase, the constraint fires itself ad infinitum. Thus, the set of constraints is not c-stratified, but is WA-stratified.   □

It is important to observe that the *WA-Str* criterion could be improved by testing safety instead of weak acyclicity over the firing graph. Further improvements could be obtained by considering super-weak acyclicity instead of safety.

Definition 5.25   [Greco et al., 2011] Given a set of TDGs Σ, we say that Σ is *SC-stratified* (*SC-Str*) if the constraints in every strongly connected component of the firing graph $\Gamma(\Sigma)$ are safe.

Moreover, we say that Σ is *SwA-stratified* (*SwA-Str*) if the constraints in every strongly connected component of the firing graph $\Gamma(\Sigma)$ are super-weak acyclic.   □

We now analyze the complexity of the above criteria starting by defining a bound on the complexity of the firing problem, i.e., the complexity of checking whether $r_1 < r_2$.

Lemma 5.26   [Greco et al., 2011] *Let $r_1 : \phi_1 \rightarrow A_1 \wedge \cdots A_k$ and $r_2 : B_1 \wedge \cdots B_n \rightarrow \psi_2$ be two TGDs. The problem of checking whether $r_1 < r_2$ is bounded by $O((k+1)^n)$.*   □

Although the theoretical complexity of the "firing" problem is exponential, in most cases it is very low (e.g., inclusion dependencies, multivalued dependencies), as usually the number n of body atoms in the fired constraint r_2 is small. Furthermore, the number of atoms in the head of constraint r_1 which could be used to fire r_2 through their unification with B_i (i.e., $k_i > 1$) is even smaller. Indeed, if the number of atoms in the body of r_2 is bounded by a constant, the firing problem is in

PTIME. In the following, for a given set of constraints Σ, we shall denote with C_{ij} the complexity of the problem of checking whether $r_i < r_j$, for $r_i, r_j \in \Sigma$, and with $C_m = max\{C_{ij}|r_i, r_j \in \Sigma\}$.

Proposition 5.27   [Greco et al., 2011] *Let Σ be a set of TGDs, D be a database Then:*

- *the problem of checking whether Σ is WA-stratified (resp. SC-stratified, SwA-stratified) is bounded by $O(C_m \times |\Sigma|^2)$;*

- *if Σ is WA-stratified (resp. SC-stratified, SwA-stratified), the length of every chase sequence of Σ over D is polynomial in the size of D.* □

As reported in the next section, the most general stratification condition defined, i.e., SwA-Str, extends SwA, but results incomparable with IR. It is trivial that more powerful criteria could be defined by composing criteria which are not comparable. We next present a different generalization of super-weak acyclicity which also generalizes the class $\mathcal{IR}$.

We start by introducing a notion of *fireable place*. We say that a place q appearing in the body of constraint r could be fired by a place q' appearing in the head of constraint r', denoted by $q' < q$, if $q \sim q'$ and $r' < r$. Given two sets of places Q and Q', we say that Q could be fired by Q', denoted by $Q' < Q$, iff for all $q \in Q$ there exists some $q' \in Q'$ such that $q' < q$.

Given a set Q of places, we define $MOVE(\Sigma, Q)$ as the smallest set of places Q' such that: (i) $Q \subseteq Q'$, and (ii) for every constraint $r = B_r \to H_r$ in $sk(\Sigma)$ and every variable x, if $Q' < \Pi_x(B_r)$, then $\Pi_x(H_r) \subseteq Q'$. Here $\Pi_x(B_r)$ and $\Pi_x(H_r)$ denote the sets of places in B_r and H_r where x occurs.

With respect to the function *Move*, the new function $MOVE$ here considered takes into account the firing of places and not only the unification of places.

Definition 5.28 (Local Stratification)   [Greco et al., 2011] Given a set Σ of TGDs and two TGDs $r_1, r_2 \in \Sigma$, we say that r_1 triggers r_2 in Σ and write $r_1 \hookrightarrow r_2$ iff there exists an existential variable y in the head of r_1, and a universal variable x occurring both in the body and head of r_2 such that $MOVE(\Sigma, Out(r_1, y)) < In(r_2, x)$. A set of constraints Σ is *locally stratified* (LS) iff the trigger graph $\Delta(\Sigma) = \{(r_1, r_2)|r_1 \hookrightarrow r_2\}$ is acyclic. □

The class of locally stratified constraints is denoted by $\mathcal{LS}$.

Example 5.29   The following set of constraints is neither in $\mathcal{IR}$ nor in $\mathcal{SwA}$-$\mathcal{Str}$, but it belongs to the class $\mathcal{LS}$:

$$r_1 : N(x) \to \exists\, y\, \exists z\, E(x, y) \wedge S(z, y)$$
$$r_2 : E(x, y) \wedge S(x, y) \to N(y)\qquad.$$
$$r_3 : E(x, y) \to E(y, x)$$

Considering SwA, we have that $Move(\Sigma, Out(r_1, y)) = \{p_3, p_5, p_{10}, p_{13}, p_2, p_{14}\}$ and $In(r_1, x) = \{p_1\} \sqsubseteq Move(\Sigma, Out(r_1, y))$. The trigger graph is cyclic as $r_1 \leadsto r_1$ and, therefore, $\Sigma_{5.29}$ is not super-weakly acyclic. As $r_1 < r_3 < r_2 < r_1$ we have that $\Sigma_{5.29}$ is not SwA-Str as well.

$\Sigma_{5.29}$ is not IR as $r_1 \prec_c r_3 \prec_c r_2 \prec_c r_1$ and for each pair of constraints r_i, r_j such that $r_i \prec_c r_j$, it is possible to construct a database containing null values in positions E_1, E_2, N_1 and S_2 such that, whenever r_i fires r_j, a null value is propagated from the head of r_i to the head of r_j.

Moreover, as $r_1 \not\mapsto r_1$ ($MOVE(\Sigma, (r_1, y)) = \{p_3, p_5, p_{13}\}$ and $In(r_1, x) = \{p_1\} \sqsubseteq MOVE(\Sigma, Out(r_1, y)))$, $\Delta(\Sigma_{5.29})$ is acyclic and, thus, $\Sigma_{5.29}$ is locally stratified. □

Proposition 5.30 [Greco et al., 2011] *For every set of TGDs Σ and for every database D:*

- *the problem of checking whether Σ is locally stratified is bounded by $O(C_m \times |\Sigma|^2)$;*

- *if Σ is locally stratified, the length of every chase sequence of Σ over D is polynomial in the size of D.* □

5.2 RELATIONSHIP AMONG CHASE TERMINATION CONDITIONS

We now analyze more deeply the relationship among the chase termination criteria proposed in the literature. The relationship among $WA, Str, CStr, SC, SR$, and IR, and between SC and SwA have already been investigated in [Deutsch et al., 2008, Greco and Spezzano, 2010, Meier et al., 2009b]. In particular, it has been shown that

- $WA \subsetneq SC, WA \subsetneq CStr$ and $CStr \nparallel SC$, i.e., the $CStr$ and SC criteria both generalize the WA criterion, but they are not comparable[1].

- $CStr \cup SC \subsetneq SR$ and $SR \subsetneq IR$, i.e., the $CStr$ and SC criteria are generalized by the SR criterion. Obviously $CStr \subsetneq Str$.

- $WA \subsetneq SC \subsetneq SwA$.

Let us start with an observation on the relationship $CStr \subsetneq SR$ by means of an example.

Example 5.31 Consider the below set of TGDs $\Sigma_{5.31}$ derived from $\Sigma_{5.9}$ by adding constraint r_2:

$$r_1 : E(x, y) \wedge E(y, x) \rightarrow \exists z \exists w \, E(y, z) \wedge E(z, w) \wedge E(w, x)$$
$$r_2 : E(x, y) \rightarrow T(x, y) \, .$$

$\Sigma_{5.31}$ is c-stratified since $G_c(\Sigma_{5.9})$ is acyclic. On the other hand, since $r_1 <_\emptyset r_2$, the minimal 2-restriction system is $(G'(\Sigma_{5.31}), P)$, where $P = \{E_1, E_2, T_1, T_2\}$, graph $G'(\Sigma_{5.31})$ contains the unique edge $\{(r_2, r_1)\}$, and its strongly connected components are $\{r_1\}$ and $\{r_2\}$. Since $\{r_1\}$ is not safe, $\Sigma_{5.31}$ is not safely restricted. □

---

[1]The notation $A \nparallel B$ is a shorthand for $A \nsubseteq B$ and $A \nsupseteq B$.

The problem in the previous example is that we should consider just *non-trivial* components (components containing at least one edge, i.e., cyclic components), as acyclic ones cannot induce infinite chase sequences. Although the formal definition of safe restriction refers to components, probably the authors referred to cyclic components. Therefore, from now on we assume that Σ is safely restricted if and only if every non-trivial strongly connected component in $G'(\Sigma)$ is safe, where $(G'(\Sigma), P)$ is the minimal 2-restriction system for Σ.

We now analyze the relationship between the above discussed classes and SwA. The below corollaries present two minor results which also have been achieved independently by Meier [2010] and Greco and Spezzano [2010].

Corollary 5.32 $SwA \nsubseteq CStr.$ □

The above result derives from the fact that the set of constraints of Example 5.9 is (c)-stratified, but not super-weakly acyclic, and from $CStr \nsubseteq SC$ and $SC \subsetneq SwA$.

Example 5.33 The following set of constraints $\Sigma_{5.33}$ is neither in $\mathcal{IR}$ nor in $\mathcal{SR}$ but it belongs to the class SwA:

$$r_1 : N(x) \rightarrow \exists y \, \exists z \, E(x, y, z)$$
$$r_2 : E(x, y, z) \rightarrow T(x, y, z) \quad .$$
$$r_3 : T(x, y, y) \rightarrow N(y)$$

Indeed, $\Sigma'_{5.33}$ is not IR (and, obviously, SR) since $r_1 <_P r_2 <_P r_3 <_P r_1$, where $P = \{E_2, E_3, T_2, T_3, N_1, E_1, T_1\}$, and the unique component is not safe (i.e., $N_1 \overset{*}{\rightarrow} E_2$, $E_2 \rightarrow T_2$, $T_2 \rightarrow N_1$). Moreover, $\Sigma_{5.33}$ is in SwA since the corresponding trigger graph is acyclic. □

Corollary 5.34 $SwA \nsubseteq SR$ and $SwA \nsubseteq \mathcal{IR}.$ □

The previous result states that super-weak acyclicity is not comparable with c-stratification and, consequently, also with the safe restriction and the inductive restriction criteria. Let's now analyze the relationships among WA-stratification, local stratification and other criteria.

The following proposition states that the WA-Str criterion is more general than $CStr$ and is not comparable with SC. Consequently, it is not comparable even with SwA as SC is strictly contained in SwA, and $CStr$ is not comparable with SwA.

Proposition 5.35 [Greco et al., 2011] $CStr \subsetneq WA$-Str and $SC \nsubseteq WA$-$Str.$ □

The next theorem states the relationships among C-Str, for $C \in \{WA, SC, SwA\}$, and other previously defined conditions.

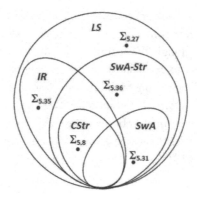

Figure 5.1: Criteria relationships.

Theorem 5.36   [Greco et al., 2011]

   1. WA-Str $\subsetneq$ SC-Str $\subsetneq$ SwA-Str;

   2. for $C \in \{WA, SC, SwA\}$, $C \subsetneq C$-Str; and

   3. SR $\nparallel$ SwA-Str and IR $\nparallel$ SwA-Str.   □

Example 5.37   Consider the below set of constraints $\Sigma_{5.37}$:

$$r_1 :\ N(x) \rightarrow \exists y\, \exists z\ E(x, y) \wedge S(z, y)$$
$$r_2 :\ E(x, y) \wedge S(x, y) \rightarrow N(y)$$
$$r_3 :\ E(x, y) \rightarrow E(x, x)\,.$$

The set $\Sigma_{5.37}$ is *SR* (and, obviously *IR*), but not *SwA-Str*. Indeed, since $r_1 < r_3 < r_2 < r_1$, we have a unique component $\{r_1, r_2, r_3\}$ which is not *SwA*.   □

Example 5.38   Consider the set of constraints $\Sigma_{5.38}$:

$$r_1 :\ N(x) \rightarrow \exists y\, \exists z\ E(x, y, z)$$
$$r_2 :\ E(x, y, z) \rightarrow T(x, y, z)$$
$$r_3 :\ T(x, y, y) \rightarrow N(y)$$
$$r_4 :\ R(x, y) \wedge R(y, x) \rightarrow \exists u\, \exists v\ R(x, u) \wedge R(u, v) \wedge R(v, x)$$

obtained as union of the set $\Sigma_{5.33} = \{r_1, r_2, r_3\}$, which is *SwA*, but not *IR*, and the set $\{r_4\}$, which is *CStr* (and, therefore, safely and inductively restricted), but not *SwA*. The set of constraints $\Sigma_{5.38}$ is neither *IR*, nor *SwA*, but it belongs to the class *SwA-Str*.   □

The below theorem states that the class of locally stratified constraints is more general than SwA-Str and IR.

Theorem 5.39   [Greco et al., 2011] SwA-$Str \subsetneq LS$ and $IR \subsetneq LS$.   □

A complete characterization of the relationships among termination condition criteria is summed up in Figure 5.1. Notice that a set of constraints Σ_i in Figure 5.1 refers to the constraints used in the correspondent Example i.

5.3   CONSTRAINT REWRITING

A technique for checking chase termination by rewriting the source set of constraints into an equivalent set has been presented by Greco and Spezzano [2010]. The technique consists of rewriting the original set of constraints Σ into an 'equivalent' set Σ^α, and verifying the structural properties for chase termination on Σ^α. The rewriting of constraints, based on the use of adornments to perform a deeper pattern analysis, allows for the reconition of larger classes of constraints for which chase termination is guaranteed: if Σ satisfies chase termination conditions C, then the rewritten set Σ^α satisfies C as well, but the reverse is not true, that is there are significant classes of constraints for which Σ^α satisfies C and Σ does not.

Before presenting the rewriting technique we introduce some definitions concerning constraints equivalence. In particular, the equivalence between two sets of constraints Σ_1 and Σ_2 defined, respectively, over two schemas $\mathbf{R}_1$ and $\mathbf{R}_2$, is given with respect to two sets of relations $R, S \subseteq \mathbf{R}_1 \cap \mathbf{R}_2$ called, respectively, input and output relations.

Let K be a database over a relational schema $\mathbf{R}$ and $S \subseteq \mathbf{R}$, then $K[S]$ denotes the subset of K consisting of instances whose predicates are in S (clearly $K = K[\mathbf{R}]$). Analogously, if we have a collection of databases $K_C = \{K_1, \dots, K_n\}$ where each K_i is defined over a schema $\mathbf{R}_i$ and let $S \subseteq \cap_{i \in [1 \dots n]} \mathbf{R}_i$, then $K_C[S] = \{K_1[S], \dots, K_n[S]\}$.

Definition 5.40   (Sets of constraints equivalence)   Given two sets of constraints Σ_1 and Σ_2 over the two database schemas $\mathbf{R}_1$ and $\mathbf{R}_2$, respectively, and two sets of relations $R, S \subseteq \mathbf{R}_1 \cap \mathbf{R}_2$, we say that $\langle \mathbf{R}_1, \Sigma_1 \rangle \sqsubseteq_{R/S} \langle \mathbf{R}_2, \Sigma_2 \rangle$ if for all database D over R, $USol(D, \Sigma_1)[S] \subseteq USol(D, \Sigma_2)[S]$. Moreover, we say that $\langle \mathbf{R}_1, \Sigma_1 \rangle$ and $\langle \mathbf{R}_2, \Sigma_2 \rangle$ are equivalent with respect to R/S and write $\langle \mathbf{R}_1, \Sigma_1 \rangle \equiv_{R/S} \langle \mathbf{R}_2, \Sigma_2 \rangle$ if both $\langle \mathbf{R}_1, \Sigma_1 \rangle \sqsubseteq_{R/S} \langle \mathbf{R}_2, \Sigma_2 \rangle$ and $\langle \mathbf{R}_2, \Sigma_2 \rangle \sqsubseteq_{R/S} \langle \mathbf{R}_1, \Sigma_1 \rangle$.   □

When $R = S = \mathbf{R}_1 \cap \mathbf{R}_2$, we simply write $\langle \mathbf{R}_1, \Sigma_1 \rangle \sqsubseteq \langle \mathbf{R}_2, \Sigma_2 \rangle$ and $\langle \mathbf{R}_1, \Sigma_1 \rangle \equiv \langle \mathbf{R}_2, \Sigma_2 \rangle$.

Example 5.41   Consider the database schema $\mathbf{R}_1 = \{E(A, B)\}$ consisting of the binary relation E and the database schema $\mathbf{R}_2 = \{E(A, B), Q(C)\}$ consisting of the binary relation E and the unary relation Q. Assume to have the following sets of TGDs:

$$\Sigma_1 = \{E(x, y) \rightarrow E(y, x)\} \text{ and}$$

$$\Sigma_2 = \{E(x, y) \rightarrow Q(x),\ \ Q(x) \wedge E(x, y) \rightarrow E(y, x)\}$$

defined over $\mathbf{R}_1$ and $\mathbf{R}_2$, respectively. Clearly, $USol(D, \Sigma_1)[E] = USol(D, \Sigma_2)[E]$ for all databases D over $\mathbf{R}_1 \cap \mathbf{R}_2 = \{E\}$ and, therefore, $\langle \mathbf{R}_1, \Sigma_1 \rangle \equiv \langle \mathbf{R}_2, \Sigma_2 \rangle$. $\square$

Adornments   An adornment α of a predicate p with arity m is a string of length m over the alphabet $\{b, f\}$. A predicate symbol p^α is said to be adorned, whereas an adorned atom is of the form $p^{\alpha_1 \cdots \alpha_m}(x_1, ..., x_m)$. If $\alpha_i = b$, we say that the variable x_i is bounded, otherwise $(\alpha_i = f)$ we say that x_i is free. Intuitively, bounded terms can take values from finite domains; consequently, constant terms are always adorned with the symbol b. If each body variable of a TGD is associated with a unique adornment, we say that the adornment of the body is *coherent*. Given a TGD $r : \phi(\mathbf{x}, \mathbf{z}) \rightarrow \exists \mathbf{y}\, \psi(\mathbf{x}, \mathbf{y})$, let α be a coherent adornment for the body atoms. $HeadAdn(r, \phi^\alpha(\mathbf{x}, \mathbf{z}))$ denotes the *adorned head* of r (with respect to the adorned body $\phi^\alpha(\mathbf{x}, \mathbf{z})$) obtained by adorning head atoms as follows: (i) every universally quantified variable has the same adornment of the body occurrences; (ii) constants are adorned as b; and (iii) existentially quantified variables are adorned as f.

Rewriting algorithm   Given a set of TGDs Σ over a schema $\mathbf{R}$, the corresponding rewriting set $Adn(\Sigma)$ consists of the union of four sets of TGDs: the base set $Base(\Sigma)$, the derived set $Derived(\Sigma)$, the input set $In(\Sigma)$, and the output set $Out(\Sigma)$.

The rewriting is performed by means of the function Adn. It starts by adorning, for each TGD, body predicates with strings of b symbols and adorning heads according to the body adornments by using the function $HeadAdn$ (base set). Next, each new adorned predicate symbol is used to generate new adorned constraints until all adorned predicate symbols are used (derived set). At the end, TGDs mapping source relations into relations adorned with strings of b symbols (input set) and TGDs mapping relations having the same predicate and different adornments into a unique relation (output set) are added.

Example 5.42   Consider the following set of constraints $\Sigma_{5.42}$:

$$\forall x\ Employee(x) \rightarrow \exists y\ WorksFor(x, y)$$
$$\forall x\, \forall y\ WorksFor(x, y) \rightarrow \exists z\ Managed(y, z)$$
$$\forall x\, \forall y\ Department(x) \wedge Managed(x, y) \rightarrow Employee(y)$$

The Adn technique starts by rewriting constraints, associating to body predicates strings of b symbols and to the head predicates, by using the function $HeadAdn$, the same body adornments for universally quantified variables, and f symbols for existentially quantified variables $(Base(\Sigma_{5.42}))$:

$$\forall x \; Employee^b(x) \to \exists y \; WorksFor^{bf}(x, y)$$
$$\forall x \; WorksFor^{bb}(x, y) \to \exists z \; Managed^{bf}(y, z)$$
$$\forall x \, \forall y \; Department^b(x) \wedge Managed^{bb}(x, y) \to Employee^b(y)$$

Subsequently, due to the new predicates $WorksFor^{bf}(x, y)$ and $Managed^{bf}(x, y)$, the rewriting continues by producing the following set of constraints ($Derived(\Sigma_{5.42})$):

$$\forall x \, \forall y \; WorksFor^{bf}(x, y) \to \exists z \; Managed^{ff}(y, z)$$
$$\forall x \, \forall y \; Department^b(x) \wedge Managed^{bf}(x, y) \to Employee^f(y)$$
$$\forall x \; Employee^f(x) \to \exists y \; WorksFor^{ff}(x, y)$$
$$\forall x \, \forall y \; WorksFor^{ff}(x, y) \to \exists z \; Managed^{ff}(y, z)$$

At this point, the rewriting terminates, since the predicate $Department^b(x)$ cannot be joined with $Managed^{ff}(x, y)$ to produce a new adorned constraints. This is because the adornment of the variable x is not coherent.

Moreover, $Adn(\Sigma_{5.42})$ also contains TGDs mapping input tuples into "bounded predicates" ($In(\Sigma_{5.42})$):

$$Employee(x) \to Employee^b(x)$$
$$Department(x) \to Department^b(x)$$
$$Managed(x, y) \to Managed^{bb}(x, y)$$
$$WorksFor(x, y) \to WorksFor^{bb}(x, y)$$

and TGDs mapping tuples of adorned relations into "output" relations ($Out(\Sigma_{5.42})$):

$$Employee^b(x) \to \hat{Employee}(x)$$
$$Employee^f(x) \to \hat{Employee}(x)$$
$$Department^b(x) \to \hat{Department}(x)$$
$$Managed^{bb}(x, y) \to \hat{Managed}(x, y)$$
$$Managed^{bf}(x, y) \to \hat{Managed}(x, y)$$
$$Managed^{ff}(x, y) \to \hat{Managed}(x, y)$$
$$WorksFor^{bb}(x, y) \to \hat{WorksFor}(x, y)$$
$$WorksFor^{bf}(x, y) \to \hat{WorksFor}(x, y)$$
$$WorksFor^{ff}(x, y) \to \hat{WorksFor}(x, y)$$

The rewritten set of constraints $Adn(\Sigma_{5.42})$ is weakly acyclic (it is sufficient to perform the test only on $Derived(\Sigma_{5.42})$), whereas the original set $\Sigma_{5.42}$ is not recognized by any chase termination criteria. $\qquad \square$

To show the equivalence between Σ and Σ^α, the following definition has been introduced. For any input database schema $\mathbf{R}$ and set of constraints Σ over $\mathbf{R}$, we denote with: (i) $\hat{\mathbf{R}} = \{\hat{p}(A_1, ..., A_n) \mid p(A_1, ..., A_n) \in \mathbf{R}\}$, the output schema derived from $\mathbf{R}$; (ii) $Adn(\mathbf{R}, \Sigma) = \mathbf{R} \cup \{p^\alpha(A_1, ..., A_n) \mid p(A_1, ..., A_n) \in \mathbf{R} \wedge p^\alpha \text{ appears in } Adn(\Sigma)\} \cup \hat{\mathbf{R}}$, the schema obtained by adding to **R** the schemas of the relations introduced in the rewriting of constraints; (iii) $Map(\mathbf{R}) = \mathbf{R} \cup \hat{\mathbf{R}}$, the union of the input and output schemas; and (iv) $Map(\Sigma) = \Sigma \cup \{p(x_1, ..., x_n) \rightarrow \hat{p}(x_1, ..., x_n)|$ $p(A_1, ..., A_n) \in \mathbf{R}\}$, the set of constraints containing, in addition to Σ, a set of TGDs mapping tuples over the input schema to tuples over the output schema.

Theorem 5.43   [Greco and Spezzano, 2010] *For every set of TGDs Σ over a database schema $\mathbf{R}$,* $\langle Map(\mathbf{R}), Map(\Sigma) \rangle \equiv_{\mathbf{R}/\hat{\mathbf{R}}} \langle Adn(\mathbf{R}, \Sigma), Adn(\Sigma) \rangle.$ □

The previous theorem states that for every database D over a schema $\mathbf{R}$ and for each universal solution J derived by applying the source TGDs Σ to D there is a universal solution K derived by applying the rewritten constraints $Adn(\Sigma)$ to D such that $J[\hat{\mathbf{R}}] = K[\hat{\mathbf{R}}]$ and vice versa.

Let $\mathcal{C}$ denote the class of TGDs satisfying criterion C, $Adn\text{-}\mathcal{C}$ denotes the class of TGDs Σ such that $Adn(\Sigma)$ satisfies criterion C. The below theorem states that the rewriting technique allows for the recognition of (by using classical criteria) larger classes of constraints for which chase termination is guaranteed.

Theorem 5.44   [Greco and Spezzano, 2010] *For any $C, C' \in \{WA, SC, CStr, SwA, SR,$ $IR, WA\text{-}Str, SC\text{-}Str, SwA\text{-}Str, LS\}$, (i) $\mathcal{C} \subsetneq Adn\text{-}\mathcal{C}$ and (ii) $\mathcal{C} \subseteq \mathcal{C}'$ implies $Adn\text{-}\mathcal{C} \subseteq Adn\text{-}\mathcal{C}'$.* □

The above theorem states that the rewriting technique allows to recognize (by using classical criteria) larger classes of constraints for which chase termination is guaranteed. From Theorem 5.43 we have that if a set of constraints $\Sigma \in Adn\text{-}\mathcal{WA}$ (resp. $Adn\text{-}\mathcal{SC}$, $Adn\text{-}\mathcal{CStr}$, $Adn\text{-}\mathcal{SwA}$, etc.) all chase sequences terminate, whereas if $\Sigma \in Adn\text{-}\mathcal{Str}$ there is at least one terminating chase sequence.

Intuitively, the advantage of adorning constraints is that atoms and constraints are "expanded" (from the same atom or dependency more adorned atoms and dependencies are derived) and the possibility that the resulting graph (based on propagation of nulls among adornments or the firing of rules) is cyclic is reduced. Indeed, considering a program P and the graph $G(P)$ used by a given criterion, if there is an edge from a node A to a node B in $G(P)$, assuming that the graph $G(Adn(P))$ contains nodes $A^{\alpha_1}, ..., A^{\alpha_b}$ and $B^{\beta_1}, ..., B^{\beta_m}$ derived, respectively, from A and B, then: (i) there will be an edge in $G(Adn(P))$ from some node A^{α_1} to some node B^{β_j}, but (ii) for each pair of nodes A^{α_1} and B^{β_j}, $G(Adn(P))$ does not necessarily contain an edge from A^{α_1} to B^{β_j}. The graph $G(P)$ can be derived from $G(Adn(P))$, by collapsing nodes having different adornments. This means that if the graph $G(Adn(P))$ is cyclic, $G(P)$ is cyclic as well, but the reverse not true. Observe also in some cases for a given recursive program P, the equivalent adorned program $Adn(P)$ is not recursive and, therefore, recognized as terminating by all criteria (see, for instance, Example 5.42).

Rewriting Algorithm Improvement.   The rewriting algorithm Adn has been further improved by the algorithm Adn^+ [Greco et al., 2011].

First of all, different types of adornments for free variables are used. In particular, instead of simply using f to denote that a position may contain null values, adornments of the form f_i are used, where the subscript i is an integer value associated to the skolem function $f_y^r(\alpha[\mathbf{x}])$ (here $\alpha[\mathbf{x}]$

denotes the substring of α corresponding to $\mathbf{x}$). In order to have a finite set of rewritten constraints, substitutions for adornments sequences are used, and a constraint r^α is added to the derived set only if there is no adorned constraint having similar structure, i.e., there is no substitution[2] θ such that $r^\alpha \theta = r^\beta$. However, if such substitution exists, the new constraint $Body(r^\alpha) \rightarrow Head(r^\beta)$ is added.

Second, in the generation of adorned predicates it is also considered how constraints may fire each other; more specifically, an adorned predicate, generated in the head of r_i^α, can be substituted in the body of an adorned constraints r_j^β to generate a new adorned constraint only if $r_i < r_j$. That is, r_i fires r_j according to the precedence relation of WA-stratification.

Finally, in addition to the adorned set of TGDs, the algorithm Adn^+ also returns a boolean value, Adn_{cyc}, taking into account the fact that a form of cyclicity has been detected in the rewriting of the constraints, and a substitution has been used to unify two adorned constraints.

Given a set of TGDs Σ over a schema $\mathbf{R}$ let $Adn^+(\Sigma)$ denote the corresponding set of TGDs obtained by rewriting Σ by means of the function Adn^+. An equivalence result, analogous to Theorem 5.43, exists for $Adn^+(\Sigma)$, i.e., for every set of TGDs Σ over a schema $\mathbf{R}$, $Adn^+(\Sigma)$ is "equivalent" to Σ with respect to $\mathbf{R}/\hat{\mathbf{R}}$ [Greco et al., 2011].

The following theorem states that the rewriting of constraints Adn^+ allows to recognize larger classes of constraints for which chase termination is guaranteed.

Theorem 5.45 [Greco et al., 2011] *For any* $C \in \{WA, SC, CStr, SwA, SR,$ $IR, WA\text{-}Str, SC\text{-}Str, SwA\text{-}Str, LS\}$, $C \subsetneq Adn\text{-}C \subsetneq Adn^+\text{-}C$. $\qquad\square$

Moreover, thanks to the boolean value Adn_{cyc} returned by the function Adn^+, a new class of constraints for which chase termination is guaranteed has been defined. This class guarantees the termination of the chase for all sequences and for all database instances D, in polynomial time in the size of D.

Definition 5.46 (Acyclicity) [Greco et al., 2011] A set of TGDs Σ is said to be *acyclic (AC)* if Adn_{cyc} is false. $\qquad\square$

The class of acyclic constraint is denoted by $\mathcal{AC}$. The next theorem shows that all criteria coincide with the criterion AC when constraints are rewritten using the adornment function Adn^+.

Theorem 5.47 [Greco et al., 2011] $\mathcal{AC} = Adn^+\text{-}\mathcal{WA} = Adn^+\text{-}\mathcal{LS}$. $\qquad\square$

To the best of our knowledge, the class of acyclic sets of constraints is the most general class guaranteeing the termination of the chase algorithm.

---

[2] A substitution θ is a set of pairs f_i/f_j such that $i \neq j$; obviously, the same symbol cannot be used in both left and right sides of substitutions, i.e., a symbol f_j used to replace a symbol f_i cannot be substituted in θ by a symbol f_k.

BIBLIOGRAPHIC NOTES

The first classes of dependencies for which it has been shown that every chase sequence terminates in PTIME in the size of the input instance are *full TGDs* [Beeri and Vardi, 1984], i.e., TGDs with no existentially quantified variables, and *acyclic sets of inclusion dependencies* [Casanova et al., 1984]. The latter set of dependencies can be described by defining a directed graph in which the nodes are the relation symbols, and such that there exists an edge from R to S whenever there is an inclusion dependency from R to S. A set of inclusion dependencies is acyclic if there is no cycle in this graph. Moreover, it has also been shown that, for full TGDs, every chase sequence has the same result.

After nearly two decades, the chase restarted to receive a lot of attention from the database community, due to is usefulness in several database applications as data exchange, data integration, etc. (cf. Chapter 8).

The class of *weakly acyclic sets of TGDs and EGDs* has been defined by Fagin et al. [2003], while simultaneously Deutsch and Tannen [2003] proposed the class of *constraints with stratified-witness*, which is a strict subset of the first class. Weak acyclicity strictly includes both sets of full TGDs and acyclic sets of inclusion dependencies.

Deutsch et al. [2008] formally proved that the problem of chase termination is undecidable, and proposed the *stratification* sufficient criterium, guaranteeing the termination of the chase. From this point on, several groups of researchers started the study of sufficient condition on chase termination.

Meier et al. [2009b] proposed the criteria of *safety, c-stratification, safe restriction, inductive restriction*, and the $\mathcal{T}$-*hierarchy*. Moreover, they adapted the above criteria to ensure the termination of at least one chase sequence but not necessarily of all. As another contribution, they studied the problem of *data-dependent chase termination*, and presented sufficient termination conditions with respect to fixed instances (see [Meier, 2010, Meier et al., 2009a] for a complete overview of all that work).

Marnette [2009] defined a criterion called *termination of the (skolem) oblivious chase (TOC)* that ensures polynomial data-complexity. As the problem of deciding whether a schema mapping satisfies the TOC criterion is only recursively enumerable, a more restrictive criterion called *super-weak acyclicity* has been identified. It can be decided in PTIME while being less restrictive than weak-acyclicity and safety. Moreover, the TOC criterion has been extended to deal with disjunctive dependencies [Marnette and Geerts, 2010].

Greco et al. proposed both sufficient criteria, such as *WA(SC, SwA)-stratification* and *local stratification*, and rewriting algorithms consisting in rewriting the original set of constraints Σ into an "equivalent," but more informative, set Σ^{α}, and verifying the structural properties for chase termination on Σ^{α} [Greco and Spezzano, 2010, Greco et al., 2011].

CHAPTER 6

Data Dependencies and Normal Forms

The chase is an important tool which was initially proposed for reasoning about data dependencies and queries in the presence of dependencies. In this chapter we study special classes of data dependencies and *normal forms* for relations. Normal forms are introduced to eliminate or minimize redundant information, that is single attribute values or tuples which can be derived from other information using dependencies. Normal forms have been studied over the last 40 years, and database books present, in the context of database design, theoretical principles, desirable properties, and algorithms for the design of good database schemas. One central issue is the logical implication between dependencies, for which the chase turns out to be a valuable tool. The motivation for discussing special classes of dependencies and normal forms here comes from recent results not provided by classical database books [Abiteboul et al., 1995, Date, 2000, Elmasri and Navathe, 2000, Garcia-Molina et al., 2009, Maier, 1983, Ramakrishnan and Gehrke, 2003, Silberschatz et al., 2010, Ullman, 1988]. We deal with dependencies defined over a single relation schema.

6.1 BASIC NOTATIONS AND TERMINOLOGY

Consider a relation schema $R(U)$ and a set Σ of dependencies over $R(U)$. We say that Σ *logically implies* a dependency σ, denoted $\Sigma \models \sigma$, iff for every relation r over $R(U)$, if $r \models \Sigma$ then $r \models \sigma$. We use Σ^+ to denote the set of all dependencies logically implied by Σ, i.e., $\Sigma^+ = \{\sigma \mid \Sigma \models \sigma\}$. Given two sets of dependencies Σ and Σ', we say that Σ logically implies Σ', denoted $\Sigma \models \Sigma'$, iff $\Sigma \models \sigma'$ for every $\sigma' \in \Sigma'$. We say that Σ and Σ' are *equivalent*, denoted $\Sigma \equiv \Sigma'$, iff $\Sigma^+ = \Sigma'^+$ (or, equivalently, $\Sigma \models \Sigma'$ and $\Sigma' \models \Sigma$). A dependency σ is *explicit* (in Σ) if $\sigma \in \Sigma$, whereas it is *implicit* (in Σ) if $\Sigma \models \sigma$, but $\sigma \notin \Sigma$. A dependency is *trivial* if any relation satisfies it.

As usual, with a slight abuse of notation, a single attribute $A \in U$ will also be used to denote the singleton set $\{A\}$. Furthermore, the concatenation XY of two sets of attributes $X \subseteq U$ and $Y \subseteq U$ is used to denote their union, i.e., $X \cup Y$; likewise, XA stands for $X \cup \{A\}$ and AB stands for $\{A\} \cup \{B\}$. Given a relation r over $R(U)$ and a set of attributes $X \subseteq U$, we use $r[X]$ to denote the relation $\pi_X r$, whereas $R[X]$ denotes the schema of $r[X]$.

One issue that is closely related to logical implication of dependencies is the development of *inference rules*, that is rules that operate at a syntactic level and allow one to derive new dependencies from a certain set of dependencies. A set of inference rules is said to be *sound* if any dependency derived by applying the inference rules is logically implied by the original set of dependencies, whereas it is said *complete* if any dependency logically implied by the original set of dependencies can be derived using the inference rules.

6.2   FUNCTIONAL DEPENDENCIES

Consider a relation schema $R(U)$. As already mentioned in Chapter 2, a *functional dependency* (FD) over $R(U)$ is an expression of the form $X \rightarrow Y$, where $X, Y \subseteq U$. A relation r over $R(U)$ *satisfies* $X \rightarrow Y$ iff for each pair of tuples $t_1, t_2 \in r$, if $t_1[X] = t_2[X]$ (i.e., the two tuples agree on the X-values), then $t_1[Y] = t_2[Y]$ (i.e., the two tuples must agree also on the Y-values). Functional dependencies can be expressed by means of full EGDs. For instance, $X \rightarrow Y$ can be expressed by means of the following full EGD:

$$\forall \mathbf{x}\, \forall \mathbf{y}_1\, \forall \mathbf{y}_2\, \forall \mathbf{z}_1\, \forall \mathbf{z}_2\ [R(\mathbf{x}, \mathbf{y}_1, \mathbf{z}_1) \wedge R(\mathbf{x}, \mathbf{y}_2, \mathbf{z}_2) \rightarrow \mathbf{y}_1 = \mathbf{y}_2],$$

where $\mathbf{x}, \mathbf{y}_1, \mathbf{y}_2, \mathbf{z}_1, \mathbf{z}_2$ are tuples of variables with $\mathbf{x}, \mathbf{y}_1$ (and $\mathbf{y}_2$), $\mathbf{z}_1$ (and $\mathbf{z}_2$) being variables corresponding to attributes $X, Y, Z = U - XY$, respectively.

Given a set $\mathcal{F}$ of functional dependencies over $R(U)$, a set of attributes $X \subseteq U$ is a *superkey* if $X \rightarrow U \in \mathcal{F}^+$ (or, equivalently, $\mathcal{F} \models X \rightarrow U$). Moreover, X is a *key* if there is no $Y \subsetneq X$ which is a superkey.

To determine whether a functional dependency is logically implied by a set of functional dependencies, the following inference rules, known as *Armstrong's axioms*, can be used [Armstrong, 1974]:

A1 (Reflexivity) For every pair X and Y such that $Y \subseteq X \subseteq U$, $X \rightarrow Y$.

A2 (Augmentation) If $X \rightarrow Y$ and $Z \subseteq U$, then $XZ \rightarrow YZ$.

A3 (Transitivity) If $X \rightarrow Y$ and $Y \rightarrow Z$, then $X \rightarrow Z$.

As stated by the next theorem, every functional dependency that is not logically implied by a given set of FDs cannot be derived by applying the axioms (soundness), and using these inference rules the complete set of FDs logically implied by the starting set can be computed (completeness).

Theorem 6.1   *Armstrong's axioms are sound and complete for FDs.*   □

Additional inference rules, immediately derivable from Armstrong's axioms, can also be used.

A4 (Union) If $X \rightarrow Y$ and $X \rightarrow Z$, then $X \rightarrow YZ$.

A5 (Decomposition) If $X \rightarrow Y$, then, for every $Z \subseteq Y$, $X \rightarrow Z$.

A6 (Pseudotransitivity) If $X \rightarrow Y$ and $YW \rightarrow Z$, then $XW \rightarrow Z$.

The closure of a set of attributes X, denoted by X^+, is the maximal set of attributes such that $\mathcal{F} \models X \to X^+$. X^+ can be easily computed by initially assigning $X^+ = X$ and iteratively adding to X^+ the set of attributes Y such that there is an FD $Z \to Y$ in $\mathcal{F}$ with $Z \subseteq X^+$. Trivial FDs are exactly those of the form $X \to Y$ where $Y \subseteq X$ (i.e., $X \to Y$ is trivial iff $Y \subseteq X$).

The equivalence $\mathcal{F} \equiv \mathcal{G}$ between two sets of FDs $\mathcal{F}$ and $\mathcal{G}$ can be checked by verifying that $\mathcal{F} \models (\mathcal{G} - \mathcal{F})$ and $\mathcal{G} \models (\mathcal{F} - \mathcal{G})$. A set of FDs is in *standard form* if every FD is of the form $X \to A$ where A is a single attribute. A set of FDs in standard form that is equivalent to a set $\mathcal{F}$ of FDs can be obtained by applying the decomposition axiom. We say that $\mathcal{F}$ is in *minimal form* if there is no FD $\sigma = X \to Y$ in $\mathcal{F}$ such that (i) $\mathcal{F} \equiv (\mathcal{F} - \{\sigma\})$ or (ii) there is a dependency $\sigma' = X \to Y'$ such that $Y' \subsetneq Y$ and $\mathcal{F} \equiv (\mathcal{F} \cup \{\sigma'\} - \{\sigma\})$, or (iii) there is a dependency $\sigma' = X' \to Y$ such that $X' \subsetneq X$ and $\mathcal{F} \equiv (\mathcal{F} \cup \{\sigma'\} - \{\sigma\})$. A set of dependencies $\mathcal{G}$ is a *minimal cover* of a set of functional dependencies $\mathcal{F}$ if $\mathcal{G} \equiv \mathcal{F}$ and $\mathcal{G}$ is in minimal form.

Example 6.2 Consider the two sets of functional dependencies $\mathcal{F} = \{A \to B, B \to C, C \to A\}$ and $\mathcal{G} = \{A \to B, B \to A, B \to C, C \to B\}$. $\mathcal{F} \equiv \mathcal{G}$ as $\mathcal{F} \models \mathcal{G} - \mathcal{F} = \{B \to A, C \to B\}$ and $\mathcal{G} \models \mathcal{F} - \mathcal{G} = \{C \to A\}$. Indeed, from $\mathcal{F}$ we have $\{B \to C, C \to A\} \models B \to A$ and $\{C \to A, A \to B\} \models C \to B$, whereas from $\mathcal{G}$ we obtain $\{C \to B, B \to A\} \models C \to A$. □

6.3 MULTIVALUED DEPENDENCIES

Consider a relation schema $R(U)$. A *multivalued dependency* (MVD) over $R(U)$ is an expression of the form $X \twoheadrightarrow Y$, where $X, Y \subseteq U$. A relation r over $R(U)$ *satisfies* $X \twoheadrightarrow Y$ iff for each pair of tuples $t_1, t_2 \in r$, if $t_1[X] = t_2[X]$, then there is a tuple $t_3 \in r$ such that $t_3[X] = t_1[X], t_3[Y] = t_1[Y]$ and $t_3[Z] = t_2[Z]$, where $Z = U - XY$ (consequently, there must also exist a tuple $t_4 \in r$ such that $t_4[X] = t_1[X], t_4[Y] = t_2[Y]$ and $t_4[Z] = t_1[Z]$). Multivalued dependencies can be expressed by means of full TGDs. A multivalued dependency $X \twoheadrightarrow Y$ can be expressed by means of a full TGD of the form:

$$\forall \mathbf{x} \forall \mathbf{y}_1 \, \forall \mathbf{y}_2 \, \forall \mathbf{z}_1 \, \forall \mathbf{z}_2 \, [R(\mathbf{x}, \mathbf{y}_1, \mathbf{z}_1) \wedge R(\mathbf{x}, \mathbf{y}_2, \mathbf{z}_2) \to R(\mathbf{x}, \mathbf{y}_1, \mathbf{z}_2)],$$

where $\mathbf{x}, \mathbf{y}_1, \mathbf{y}_2, \mathbf{z}_1, \mathbf{z}_2$ are tuples of variables with $\mathbf{x}, \mathbf{y}_1$ (and $\mathbf{y}_2$), $\mathbf{z}_1$ (and $\mathbf{z}_2$) being variables corresponding to attributes $X, Y, Z = U - XY$, respectively.

Multivalued dependencies generalize functional dependencies in the sense that, as we shall see in the following, whenever an FD $X \to Y$ is satisfied, the MVD $X \twoheadrightarrow Y$ is satisfied as well, but their structure is different as they define conditions on tuples (using TGDs), whereas FDs express conditions on attribute values (using EGDs).

To determine whether an MVD is logically implied by other MVDs the following inference rules for MVDs are used.

M0 (Complementation for MVDs) If $X \twoheadrightarrow Y$, then $X \twoheadrightarrow U - XY$.

M1 (Reflexivity for MVDs) For every pair X and Y such that $Y \subseteq X \subseteq U$, then, $X \twoheadrightarrow Y$.

M2 (Augmentation for MVDs) If $X \twoheadrightarrow Y$ and $Z \subseteq U$, then $X Z \twoheadrightarrow Y Z$.

M3 (Transitivity for MVDs) If $X \twoheadrightarrow Y$ and $Y \twoheadrightarrow Z$, then $X \twoheadrightarrow Z - Y$.

Theorem 6.3   *Inference rules M0, M1, M2, M3 for MVDs are sound and complete.*   □

To determine whether an FD or an MVD is logically implied by other FDs and MVDs, in addition to the inference rules for FDs and MVDs (with the exception of M1), the following inference rules for FDs and MVDs must also be considered:

FM1 (Conversion) If $X \rightarrow Y$, then $X \twoheadrightarrow Y$.

FM2 (Interaction) If $X \twoheadrightarrow Y$ and $X Y \rightarrow Z$, then $X \rightarrow (Z - Y)$.

Theorem 6.4   *Inference rules F1, F2, F3, M0, M2, M3, FM1, FM2 are sound and complete for FDs and MVDs.*   □

Observe that axiom M1 is not necessary when inference rules for FDs and MVDs are considered together; this is because it is implied by axioms F1 and FM1. Trivial MVDs are exactly those of the form $X \twoheadrightarrow Y$ where $Y \subseteq X$ or $X Y = U$ (i.e. $X \twoheadrightarrow Y$ is trivial iff $Y \subseteq X$ or $X Y = U$).

Consider a set $\mathcal{F}$ of FDs and a set $\mathcal{M}$ of MVDs over $R(U)$, and let $\Sigma = \mathcal{F} \cup \mathcal{M}$. We say that Σ is in *minimal form* if (i) there is no $\sigma \in \Sigma$ s.t. $\Sigma \equiv \Sigma - \{\sigma\}$, and (ii) $\mathcal{F}$ is in minimal form. An MVD $X \twoheadrightarrow Y$ in Σ is *pure* if it is non-trivial and neither $X \rightarrow Y$ nor $X \rightarrow (U - XY)$ is in Σ^{+}. Σ is *pure* if every MVD in Σ is pure. Thus, if an MVD $X \twoheadrightarrow Y$ is not pure, then it follows from the inference rules that an equivalent set of dependencies can be obtained by replacing $X \twoheadrightarrow Y$ with either $X \rightarrow Y$ or $X \rightarrow (U - XY)$. Pure covers can be obtained by replacing MVDs which are not pure with FDs.

6.4   JOIN DEPENDENCIES

Consider a relation schema $R(U)$. A *join dependency* (JD) over $R(U)$ is an expression of the form $\bowtie\{X_1, ..., X_n\}$, where $X_i \subseteq U$ for $1 \leq i \leq n$, and $\bigcup_{i=1}^{n} X_i = U$. Each X_i is called a *component* of the JD. A relation r over $R(U)$ *satisfies* $\bowtie\{X_1, ..., X_n\}$ iff $r = \bowtie_{i=1}^{n} r[X_i]$.

Join dependencies generalize MVDs as any MVD $X \twoheadrightarrow Y$ can be expressed as a join dependency of the form $\bowtie \{XY, X(U - XY)\}$. Observe also that, for any partition of U into X, Y, and Z, given a set Σ of FDs and JDs, it holds $\Sigma \models \bowtie \{XY, XZ\}$ iff either $\Sigma \models X \rightarrow Y$ or $\Sigma \models X \rightarrow Z$.

Join dependencies can be expressed by means of full TGDs. For instance, the join dependency $\bowtie \{X Y, Y Z, X Z\}$ can be expressed by means of a full TGD of the form:

$$\forall x_1 \, \forall x_2 \, \forall y_1 \, \forall y_2 \, \forall z_1 \, \forall z_2 \, [R(x_1, y_1, z_2) \wedge R(x_2, y_1, z_1) \wedge R(x_1, y_2, z_1) \rightarrow R(x_1, y_1, z_1)],$$

where $\mathbf{x}_1, \mathbf{x}_2, \mathbf{y}_1, \mathbf{y}_2, \mathbf{z}_1, \mathbf{z}_2$ are tuples of variables with $\mathbf{x}_1$ (and $\mathbf{x}_2$), $\mathbf{y}_1$ (and $\mathbf{y}_2$), $\mathbf{z}_1$ (and $\mathbf{z}_2$) being variables corresponding to attributes X, Y, Z, respectively. A JD $\bowtie \{X_1, ..., X_n\}$ is trivial iff there exists a component $X_i = U$.

The following theorem states that, in contrast to FDs and MVDs, there are not sound and complete inference rules for JDs.

Theorem 6.5   [Petrov, 1989] *There is no axiomatization for join dependencies.*   □

An algorithm to check whether a join dependency σ is implied by a set of key dependencies $\mathcal{K}$ has been proposed by Fagin [1979]. The input of the algorithm is a set of key dependencies $\mathcal{K}$ and a join dependency $\sigma = \bowtie \{X_1, ..., X_n\}$. The algorithm starts by defining $S = \{X_1, ..., X_n\}$. Then, at each step it picks a key dependency $K_i \rightarrow U$ in $\mathcal{K}$ and a pair of elements $X_j, X_h \in S$ such that $K_i \subseteq (X_j \cap X_h)$, and replaces X_j and X_h with $X_j X_h$. If the algorithm terminates with $S = \{U\}$ (a single element consisting of the set of all attributes), then the algorithm succeeds, otherwise, it fails. If the algorithm succeeds, then $\mathcal{K} \models \sigma$, otherwise $\mathcal{K} \not\models \sigma$.

Example 6.6   Consider a relation schema $R(A, B, C, D)$ and a set of dependencies $\mathcal{F} \cup \mathcal{J}$, where $\mathcal{F} = \{A \rightarrow ABCD, B \rightarrow ABCD\}$ and $\mathcal{J} = \{\bowtie\{AB, AD, BC\}\}$. Suppose we want to check if $\mathcal{F} \models \mathcal{J}$, that is if the join dependency is logically implied by the functional dependencies $\mathcal{F}$. Initially, $S = \{AB, AD, BC\}$. Considering the key dependency $A \rightarrow ABCD$, the two sets AB and AD in S (which share the key A) are merged and we obtain $S = \{ABD, BC\}$. Considering now the key dependency $B \rightarrow ABCD$, we obtain $S = \{ABCD\}$. As S contains one single element corresponding to all the attributes of the schema, the join dependency is logically implied by the FDs.

Consider now a relation schema $R(ABC)$ and a set of dependencies $\mathcal{F}' \cup \mathcal{J}'$ where $\mathcal{F}' = \{A \rightarrow BC, B \rightarrow AC\}$ and $\mathcal{J}' = \{\bowtie \{AC, BC\}\}$. The set $S = \{AC, BC\}$ does not change as there are no two elements sharing a key. Therefore, $\mathcal{F}' \not\models \mathcal{J}'$.   □

Considering only two join dependencies $j_1 = \bowtie \{X_1, ..., X_m\}$ and $j_2 = \bowtie \{Y_1, ..., Y_n\}$, we have that j_1 implies j_2 iff for every X_i there exists an Y_j such that $X_i \subseteq Y_j$. A join dependency j_2 is *minimal* if there is no join dependency j_1 which implies j_2.

Example 6.7   Consider the join dependencies $j_1 = \bowtie \{AB, AC\}$ and $j_2 = \bowtie \{AB, AC, BC\}$. Since $\{AB, AC\} \subset \{AB, AC, BC\}$, j_1 implies j_2.   □

6.5 DECOMPOSITIONS

In order to minimize or eliminate possible redundant information, *normal forms* have been introduced. Relations not satisfying criteria imposed by normal forms are decomposed. For ease of presentation, in the rest of this chapter we consider a relation schema as a pair $(R(U), \Sigma)$, where $R(U)$ is a relation schema as defined in Chapter 2 (i.e., R is a relation name and U is a set of attributes) and Σ is a set of dependencies over $R(U)$. We restrict ourselves to functional and join dependencies. Thus, whenever we refer to a schema $(R(U), \Sigma)$, Σ is understood to be a set of functional/join dependencies, and when we refer to a dependency σ, it is either a functional or a join dependency, unless otherwise specified. Moreover, when we say that r is a relation over $(R(U), \Sigma)$ we mean that r is a relation over relation schema $R(U)$, as defined in Chapter 2 and r satisfies Σ. Given a set of attributes $U_i \subseteq U$, we use $\pi_{U_i}(\Sigma)$ to denote the dependencies in Σ^+ referring only to attributes in U_i.

A *decomposition* of a relation schema $(R(U), \Sigma)$ is a set of relation schemas $\{(R_1(U_1), \Sigma_1), \ldots, (R_n(U_n), \Sigma_n)\}$ such that (i) $\bigcup_{i=1}^{n} U_i = U$ and (ii) $\Sigma_i = \pi_{U_i}(\Sigma)$. Such a decomposition is denoted as $\Delta = \{U_1, \ldots, U_n\}$.

Lossless-Join decomposition.   Consider a decomposition $\Delta = \{U_1, \ldots, U_n\}$ of a relation schema $(R(U), \Sigma)$ and a relation r over $(R(U), \Sigma)$. We define $m_\Delta r = r[U_1] \bowtie \cdots \bowtie r[U_n] = \bowtie_{i=1}^{n} r[U_i]$. We say that Δ is *lossless-join* if $r = m_\Delta r$ for every relation r over $(R(U), \Sigma)$. Observe that, in general, the following properties hold: (i) $r \subseteq m_\Delta r$; (ii) if $r_1 \subseteq r_2$, then $m_\Delta r_1 \subseteq m_\Delta r_2$ (monotonicity); (iii) $m_\Delta r = m_\Delta(m_\Delta r)$ (idempotence).

The test for lossless-join decomposition can be done by applying the chase algorithm presented in Chapter 3. More specifically, given a relation schema $(R(A_1, \ldots, A_m), \mathcal{F})$, where $\mathcal{F}$ is a set of functional dependencies, and a decomposition $\Delta = \{U_1, \ldots, U_n\}$, a tableau T (that is a table containing distinguished and non-distinguished variables) with n rows and m columns is built. Each element T_{ij} is equal to α_j (assumed to be a distinguished variable) if attribute A_j is in U_i, otherwise is equal to β_{ij} (assumed to be a non-distinguished variable). At each step the chase algorithm selects a functional dependency $X \to Y$ which is not satisfied by two tuples v and w of T (i.e., such that $v[X] = w[X]$ and $v[Y] \neq w[Y]$) and at least one of the two values $v[Y]$ and $w[Y]$ is a non-distinguished variable. Assuming that $v[Y] = \beta_{ij}$ is a non-distinguished variable, the application of the functional dependency consists in replacing variable β_{ij} with $w[Y]$ everywhere in T. If the resulting tableau contains a row $(\alpha_1, \ldots, \alpha_m)$, then the decomposition is lossless-join. Moreover, for binary decompositions $\Delta = \{U_1, U_2\}$ of $(R(U), \mathcal{F})$, checking whether Δ is lossless-join can be easily done by verifying if at least one of the following conditions holds: (i) $\mathcal{F} \models (U_1 \cap U_2) \to U_1$ and (ii) $\mathcal{F} \models (U_1 \cap U_2) \to U_2$ [Aho et al., 1979a]. The formal definition of the chase algorithm applied to tableau will be presented in Section 6.7.

Lossless-FD decomposition.   Consider a decomposition $\Delta = \{U_1, \ldots, U_n\}$ of a relation schema $(R(U), \mathcal{F})$ where $\mathcal{F}$ is a set of functional dependencies. We say that Δ is *lossless-FD* (that is a decomposition preserving functional dependencies) iff $\pi_{U_1}(\mathcal{F}) \cup \cdots \cup \pi_{U_n}(\mathcal{F}) \equiv \mathcal{F}$.

Example 6.8   Consider the relation schema $(R(A, B, C), \mathcal{F})$, where $\mathcal{F} = \{A \rightarrow C, B \rightarrow C\}$), and the decompositions $\Delta_1 = \{AC, BC\}$, $\Delta_2 = \{AB, BC\}$, and $\Delta_3 = \{AB, AC, BC\}$.

Decomposition $\Delta_1 = \{AC, BC\}$ is lossless-FD as both functional dependencies in $\mathcal{F}$ are preserved in the decomposed schema. However, Δ_1 is not lossless-join as the application of the chase to $(T_1, \mathcal{F})$, where T_1 is the tableau $\{(\alpha_1, \beta_{12}, \alpha_3), (\beta_{21}, \alpha_2, \alpha_3)\}$, does not produce a tableau having a row with only distinguished variables.

Decomposition $\Delta_2 = \{AB, BC\}$ is not lossless-FD as the functional dependency $A \rightarrow C$ is not preserved in the decomposed schema. However, Δ_2 is lossless-join as the application of the chase to $(T_2, \mathcal{F})$, where $T_2 = \{(\alpha_1, \alpha_2, \beta_{13}), (\beta_{21}, \alpha_2, \alpha_3)\}$, produces the tableau $T_2^* = \{(\alpha_1, \alpha_2, \alpha_3), (\beta_{21}, \alpha_2, \alpha_3)\}$ having a row $(\alpha_1, \alpha_2, \alpha_3)$ of distinguished variables.

Decomposition $\Delta_3 = \{AB, AC, BC\}$ is lossless-FD as both functional dependencies in $\mathcal{F}$ are preserved in the decomposed schema. Moreover, Δ_3 is lossless-join as the application of the chase to $(T_3, \mathcal{F})$, where $T_3 = \{(\alpha_1, \alpha_2, \beta_{13}), (\alpha_1, \beta_{12}, \alpha_3), (\beta_{21}, \alpha_2, \alpha_3)\}$, produces the tableau $T_3^* = \{(\alpha_1, \alpha_2, \alpha_3), (\alpha_1, \beta_{12}, \alpha_3), (\beta_{21}, \alpha_2, \alpha_3)\}$ having a row $(\alpha_1, \alpha_2, \alpha_3)$.   □

6.6   NORMAL FORMS

We present normal forms, that is, desirable criteria which should be satisfied by relation schemas to avoid (or minimize) redundant information. In the following, we use Σ to denote a set of functional and join dependencies. Moreover, we use $\mathcal{F}$ (resp. $\mathcal{J}, \mathcal{K}, \mathcal{M}$) to denote a set of functional (resp. join, key, multivalued) dependencies only.

Tuple redundancy.   Consider a relation schema $(R(U), \Sigma)$. We say that a set of tuples S *logically implies* a tuple t with respect to $(R(U), \Sigma)$ if for every relation r over $(R(U), \Sigma)$, if r contains S then it also contains t (recall that a relation over $(R(U), \Sigma)$ must satisfy Σ).

Given a relation r over $(R(U), \Sigma)$, a tuple $t \in r$ is *partly redundant* if some attribute value $t[A_i]$ can be derived, using data dependencies, from the other information stored in r, that is if there is a tuple $t' \in r - \{t\}$ and a non-trivial (implicit or explicit) FD $X \rightarrow A \in \Sigma^+$, such that $t[X] = t'[X]$. A tuple $t \in r$ is *fully redundant* if the entire tuple can be derived from the knowledge of $r - \{t\}$, using data dependencies. Logical implication can be performed chasing (Σ, r). A tuple in r is *essential* if it is neither partly nor fully redundant.

Boyce-Codd normal form and FDs.   In the presence of functional dependencies several normal forms have been defined, such as second normal form (2NF), third normal form (3NF), and Boyce-Codd normal form (BCNF). As 2NF and 3NF do not guarantee that relations do not have partly redundant tuples, we only consider BCNF.

Given a relation schema $(R(U), \Sigma)$, we say that a (functional/join) dependency σ is *logically implied by the keys*, if σ is logically implied by the set of FDs in Σ^+ of the form $K \to U$, where K is a key of $(R(U), \Sigma)$.

Definition 6.9   We say that a relation schema $(R(U), \Sigma)$ is in Boyce-Codd normal form (BCNF) if every (explicit or implicit) FD in Σ^+ is logically implied by the keys.   □

As any non-trivial FD $X \to Y$ is logically implied by the keys if and only if X is a superkey [Fagin, 1979], we have the following result, which is an alternative definition of BCNF.

Proposition 6.10   *A relation schema $(R(U), \Sigma)$ is in BCNF if for each (explicit or implicit) non-trivial FD $X \to Y$ in Σ^+, X is a superkey.*   □

Observe that when Σ consists of functional dependencies only, the definition above is equivalent to the classical definition found in textbooks, saying that a relation schema $(R(U), \mathcal{F})$, where $\mathcal{F}$ is a set of functional dependencies, is in BCNF if for each (explicit) non-trivial FD $X \to Y$, X is a superkey [Silberschatz et al., 2010]. Observe also that, as join dependencies can be used to infer further functional dependencies, it is necessary to consider implicit dependencies as well. For instance, consider a relation schema $(R(A, B, C), \mathcal{F} \cup \mathcal{J})$, where $\mathcal{F} = \{AB \to C\}$ (hence AB is the only key) and $\mathcal{J} = \{\bowtie \{AB, AC\}\}$. As the join dependency is equivalent to the multivalued dependency $A \twoheadrightarrow B$, we derive the FD $A \to C$ from $A \twoheadrightarrow B$ and $AB \to C$ by applying inference rule FM2. Therefore, $(R(A, B, C), \mathcal{F} \cup \mathcal{J})$ is not in BCNF.

Proposition 6.11   [Darwen et al., 2012] *A relation schema $(R(U), \Sigma)$ is in BCNF if and only if no relation over $(R(U), \Sigma)$ has a partly redundant tuple.*   □

The proposition above states that a relation schema $(R(U), \Sigma)$ in BCNF cannot contain redundant information derivable from (explicit or implicit) FDs, that is, it is in BCNF if and only if no relation over $(R(U), \Sigma)$ has a tuple which is partly redundant with respect to the explicit and implicit functional dependencies.

Fourth normal form and MVDs.   The BCNF guarantees that relations do not have partially redundant tuples, but does not guarantee, in the presence of MVDs or JDs, that relations do not have fully redundant tuples.

Example 6.12   Consider a relation schema $(R(A, B, C), \{AB \to C, \ C \twoheadrightarrow B\})$ which can be easily verified to be in BCNF as AB is a key. Nevertheless, the relation $r = \{(a_1, b_1, c_1), (a_1, b_2, c_1), (a_2, b_1, c_1), (a_2, b_2, c_1)\}$ over the previous schema has redundant tuples. For instance, the tuples (a_1, b_1, c_1) and (a_2, b_2, c_1) are implied by the tuples (a_1, b_2, c_1) and (a_2, b_1, c_1) (using the MVD $C \twoheadrightarrow B$) and vice versa.   □

Therefore, in the presence of MVDs (or JDs) the Boyce-Codd normal form is not satisfactory. The fourth normal form extends the BCNF by also considering MVDs.

Definition 6.13 A relation schema $(R(U), \Sigma)$ is in *fourth normal form* (4NF) if each (explicit or implicit) non-trivial MVD $X \twoheadrightarrow Y$ in Σ^+ is logically implied by the keys. $\qquad \square$

Analogously to the BCNF, we have the following results which is an alternative definition of 4NF.

Proposition 6.14 *A relation schema $(R(U), \Sigma)$ is in 4NF if for each (explicit or implicit) non-trivial MVD $X \twoheadrightarrow Y$ in Σ^+, X is a superkey.* $\qquad \square$

Example 6.15 Consider the relation schema $(R(A, B, C), \{AB \to C, C \twoheadrightarrow B\})$. Such a relation schema is not in 4NF as the MVD $C \twoheadrightarrow B$ is not implied by the keys. On the other hand, the relation schema $(R(A, B, C), \{AB \to C, B \to A, B \twoheadrightarrow C\})$ is in 4NF as the MVD $B \twoheadrightarrow C$ is implied by the (implicit) key dependency $B \to AC$. $\qquad \square$

Proposition 6.16 *(4NF $\Rightarrow$ BCNF) If a relation schema $(R(U), \Sigma)$, where Σ consists only of FDs and MVDs, is in 4NF, then $(R(U), \Sigma)$ is in BCNF (with respect to the set of FDs implied by Σ).* $\qquad \square$

Beyond 4NF and JDs. The fourth normal guarantees that relations do not have partially and fully redundant tuples in the presence of FDs and MVDs, but it does not guarantee that this property holds when JDs are considered too. This is shown in the following example.

Example 6.17 Consider the relation schema $(R(A, B, C), \{ \bowtie\{AB, BC, AC\} \})$, which is in 4NF as the set of FDs and MVDs is empty. However, the relation schema does not guarantee that relations over it do not contain redundant tuples. As an example, the relation $r = \{(a, b, c'), (a', b, c), (a, b', c), (a, b, c)\}$ satisfies the join dependency $\bowtie\{AB, BC, AC\}$, but contains redundant tuples, as the tuple (a, b, c) is implied by the other three tuples. $\qquad \square$

Several normal forms have been proposed for join dependencies. Maier [1983] presents two different definitions of *project-join normal form* in his textbook—the *fifth normal form* is never mentioned, although it is understood that the final definition is the second one (called revised). The two definitions have introduced a bit of confusion. Thus, some works have assumed as distinct the two different definitions, referred to as *fifth normal form* (5NF) and *project-join normal form* (PJ/NF) [Vincent, 1997], respectively, whereas other works have considered only one normal form, and used both names to denote it [Darwen et al., 2012, Fagin, 1979]. We follow the second approach and consider only one normal form referred to as 5NF or PJ/NF.

Definition 6.18   A relation schema $(R(U), \Sigma)$ is in *fifth normal form* (5NF), a.k.a. *project-join normal form* (PJ/NF), if every (explicit or implicit) JD in Σ^+ is logically implied by the keys of R. □

The main motivation for introducing the 5NF is to extend the 4NF to consider also join dependencies. The definition of the 5NF implies that relations in 5NF are also in 4NF (5NF $\Rightarrow$ 4NF). As said above, an MVD $X \twoheadrightarrow Y$ over a relation schema $R(U)$ can be expressed as a (non-trivial) JD $\bowtie \{XY, XZ\}$, where $Z = U - XY$. It holds that a relation schema $(R(U), \Sigma)$ is in 4NF if for each MVD $\bowtie \{XY, XZ\}$, every component of the join dependency is a superkey of R. This property cannot be generalized to relations in 5NF, as shown in the following example.

Example 6.19   Consider a relation schema $(R(A, B, C), \{ AB \to C, BC \to A, AC \to B, \bowtie \{AB, AC, BC\} \})$ which is not in 5NF as it has three alternative keys (namely, AB, BC and AC), and the join dependency is not implied by the keys. However, any relation over the aforementioned schema does not have fully redundant tuples. As an example, consider a relation $r = \{(a, b, c'), (a, b', c), (a', b, c), (a, b, c)\}$ having a fully redundant tuple (in fact, the tuple (a, b, c) is implied by the other three tuples). The relation does not satisfy the FD $AB \to C$. □

The problem with the 5NF, illustrated in the previous example, is that it does not admit relations with non-trivial JDs, having superkeys as components, which are not implied by the key dependencies. Thus, further normal forms have been recently proposed.

Consider a relation schema $(R(U), \Sigma)$. A JD $\bowtie \{U_1, ..., U_n\}$ in Σ is *irreducible* if there is no proper subset $\{U_{i_1}, ..., U_{i_m}\} \subsetneq \{U_1, ..., U_n\}$ such that $\bowtie \{U_{i_1}, ..., U_{i_m}\}$ is a JD (explicit or implicit) in Σ^+.

Definition 6.20   [Normann, 1998] A relation schema $(R(U), \Sigma)$ is in *superkey normal form* (SKNF) if every component of every irreducible JD (explicit or implicit) in Σ^+ is a superkey.   □

The definition of SKNF is similar to the first definition of PJ/NF provided by Maier [1983], but SKNF considers only irreducible JDs. SKNF is also equivalent to the *reduced fifth normal form* (5NFR) proposed by Vincent [1997]. As an example, the relation schema of Example 6.19 is in superkey normal form as all components in the join dependency are superkeys. Clearly, SKNF $\Rightarrow$ 4NF (as MVDs are irreducible JDs), and 5NF $\Rightarrow$ SKNF. Moreover, as shown by Example 6.19, the reverse implication does not hold. The next example shows that even the SKNF is not satisfactory.

Example 6.21   Let $(R(A, B, C), \{ AB \to C, AC \to B, \bowtie \{AB, AC, BC\}\})$ be a relation schema. It can be easily verified that it is not in SKNF, and, consequently, not even in 5NF. Indeed, R has two alternative keys (namely, AB and AC), but the component BC of the join dependency is not a superkey. However, it can be verified that every relation over the afore-mentioned schema cannot have fully redundant tuples. As an example, consider the relation $r = \{(a, b, c'), (a, b', c), (a', b, c), (a, b, c)\}$, that has a fully redundant tuple. The relation does not actually satisfy $AB \rightarrow C$.   □

Definition 6.22   Let $(R(U), \Sigma)$ be a relation schema. A JD $\bowtie\{X_1, ..., X_p\}$ in Σ is *key-complete* (KC) if the union of its components that are superkeys is equal to U.

Example 6.23   Consider the relation schema $(R(A, B, C, D), \Sigma)$ with $\Sigma = \{A \rightarrow BCD, B \rightarrow ACD, \bowtie\{AB, BC, CD\}\}$. The JD $\bowtie\{AB, BC, ACD\}$ is implied by Σ and is KC since every component is a superkey, and their union is equal to $ABCD$. However, the JD $\bowtie\{AB, BC, CD\}$ is not KC since CD is not a superkey.   □

We now introduce a syntactic normal form based on this property.

Definition 6.24   Let $(R(U), \Sigma)$ be a relation schema where Σ is a set of FDs and JDs. Such a relation schema is in *key-complete normal form* (KCNF) if the left-hand side of every non-trivial FD in Σ is a superkey, and every JD in Σ is KC.

Thus, a relation schema is in KCNF if it is in BCNF, and for every (explicit or implicit) JD, the union of the components that are superkeys contains all the attributes of the schema. As an example, the relation schema of Example 6.21 is in KCNF, but not in SKNF.

Example 6.25   Consider now a relation schema $(R(A, B, C), \{AB \rightarrow C, \bowtie\{AB, BC, AC\}\})$, which is not in KCNF as it has only one key (namely AB), and the union of all components in the JD that are superkeys is not equal to ABC. Nevertheless, also in this case, every relation over the aforementioned schema cannot contain fully redundant tuples. For instance, the relation $r = \{(a, b, c'), (a', b, c), (a, b', c), (a, b, c)\}$ (which has a fully redundant tuple) does not satisfy the functional dependency $AB \rightarrow C$ as $c \neq c'$, whereas the relation $r = \{(a, b, c), (a', b, c), (a, b', c)\}$ is consistent (even the JD is satisfied) and does not have fully redundant tuples.   □

The previous example also shows that the KCNF is not the ultimate normal form to guarantee that relations do not present redundancies. Next we present a further normal form which naturally extends 4NF, but is less restrictive of KCNF.

Definition 6.26   [Darwen et al., 2012] A relation schema is in ETNF if every tuple in every relation over the schema is essential.   □

Theorem 6.27   [Darwen et al., 2012] *A relation schema $(R(U), \Sigma)$ is in essential tuple normal form (ETNF) if and only if it is in BCNF and some component of every explicit JD in Σ is a superkey.*   □

The relation schema of Example 6.25 is in ETNF, as it is in BCNF and there is a component of the join dependency containing the key AB.

Considering the complete framework of the aforementioned normal forms, we have that $5NF \Rightarrow SKNF \Rightarrow KCNF \Rightarrow ETNF \Rightarrow 4NF \Rightarrow BCNF$, and none of the reverse implications holds (Darwen et al. [2012]).

As we have seen, the chase algorithm is an important tool which can also be used for checking whether a decomposition is lossless-join. Although the chase algorithm informally presented in Section 6.5 is applied to tableau, it works as the one presented in Section 4.1, which is applied to databases. The next section shows that the chase algorithm can be used to check whether a given dependency is logically implied by a set dependencies.

6.7 CHASING WITH FDS AND JDS

Although for FDs and JDs we do not have a sound and complete set of inference rules, it is possible to check whether a given dependency σ is logically implied by a set of dependencies Σ, that is whether σ belongs to Σ^+. This can be carried out by building specific tableau and applying the chase algorithm over such tableau. Restricting dependencies to FDs and JDs, at most one distinguished variable may appear in any column and, by convention, the distinguished variable associated with a column A_i is denoted by α_i. The chase algorithm adds new tuples of variables and replaces non-distinguished variables. Analogously to the chase algorithm considered in Section 4.1, the chase algorithm used here performs a sort of tableau completions where new tuples can be added and non-distinguished variables can be replaced by other variables (equivalent to saying that labeled nulls can be replaced by constants or by other labeled nulls); distinguished variables cannot be replaced (equivalent to saying that constants cannot be replaced). By convention, if two non-distinguished variables β_i and β_j, with $i < j$, must be equal, then β_j is replaced by β_i.

Thus, the problem is, given a relation schema $(R(U), \Sigma)$ and a dependency σ, to check whether $\Sigma \models \sigma$. To answer this question, a tableau T is built, considering the type and the structure of σ. Then, it is checked whether the tableau T^*, obtained through the application of the chase algorithm to T and Σ, contains a specific tuple. As we will see, non-distinguished variables occur at most once in the starting relation r, whereas a distinguished variable occurs only in one column, and each column contains at most one distinguished variable. The aforementioned tableau T is built as follows (as already mentioned, we consider two different cases according to the type of dependency σ):

- $\sigma = X \to Y$ and $U = XYZ$. Take the tableau T containing the two tuples $(\alpha_1, \alpha_2, \alpha_3)$ and $(\alpha_1, \beta_2, \beta_3)$, where $\alpha_1, \alpha_2, \alpha_3$ (resp. β_2, β_3) are tuples of distinguished (resp. non-distinguished) variables corresponding to attributes X, Y, Z (resp. Y, Z), respectively. If the result of the chase algorithm is a tableau (possibly with additional tuples), where β_2 has been replaced by α_2, then $\Sigma \models X \to Y$.

- $\sigma = \bowtie \{X_1, \ldots, X_p\}$. Take the tableau T containing p tuples, such that for each $i \in [1..p]$, there is a tuple where the value of each attribute $A_j \in X_i$ is α_j, and the values of the remaining attributes A_k are non-distinguished variables β_{i_k} occurring once in the tableau. If the result of the chase algorithm is a tableau having a tuple where the value of each attribute $A_j \in (X_1 \cup \cdots \cup X_p)$ is α_j, then $\Sigma \models \sigma$.

Notice that the chase steps are applied as defined in Chapter 4, and FDs act as EGDs and JDs as TGDs.

Example 6.28   Consider the relation schema $(R(A, B, C), \Sigma)$, where $\Sigma = \{AB \to C, \bowtie \{AB, AC\}\})$, and the FD $\sigma = A \to C$. To check whether $\Sigma \models \sigma$ we build the tableau $T = \{(\alpha_1, \alpha_2, \alpha_3), (\alpha_1, \beta_2, \beta_3)\}$, and chase T with Σ. By chasing with respect to the JD we obtain the relation $T' = \{(\alpha_1, \alpha_2, \alpha_3), (\alpha_1, \beta_2, \beta_3), (\alpha_1, \alpha_2, \beta_3), (\alpha_1, \beta_2, \alpha_3)\}$. From the application of the functional dependency we derive tableau $T^* = \{(\alpha_1, \alpha_2, \alpha_3), (\alpha_1, \beta_2, \alpha_3)\}$. As β_3 has been replaced by α_3, it follows $\Sigma \models A \to C$.

Consider now the relation schema $(R(A, B, C), \Sigma)$, where $\Sigma = \{A \to B\}$, and $\sigma = \bowtie \{AB, AC\}$. First, $T = \{(\alpha_1, \alpha_2, \beta_3), (\alpha_1, \beta_2, \alpha_3)\}$. By chasing with respect to the FD we get the relation $T^* = \{(\alpha_1, \alpha_2, \beta_3), (\alpha_1, \alpha_2, \alpha_3)\}$. Since we derived a row with only distinguished variables, we have that $\{A \to B\} \models \bowtie \{AB, AC\}$.   □

Observe that in the previous example we have considered JDs that are MVDs and that the two chase applications correspond to the application of axioms FM1 and FM2 of Section 6.3, respectively.

The relation between JDs and MVDs is not limited to binary JDs (MVDs are binary JDs). Let us first recall the definition of hypergraph and path over a hypergraph. A hypergraph is a generalization of a graph in which an edge can connect any number of vertices. More formally, a hypergraph H is a pair (V, E) where V is a set of nodes and $E \subseteq 2^V$ is a set of edges. Here 2^V denotes the powerset of V, that is the set of all subsets of V. Clearly, each edge $e \in E$ must be a nonempty subset of V. A path p in H is a sequence of edges $e_1, e_2, \ldots, e_n$ of H such that $e_i \cap e_{i+1} \neq \emptyset$, for $1 \leq i < n$; p defines a cycle if $e_n \cap e_1 \neq \emptyset$.

A join dependency $\bowtie \{X_1, \ldots, X_p\}$ is said to be *acyclic* if the hypergraph with edges $X_1, \ldots, X_p$ is acyclic.

Proposition 6.29   [Maier et al., 1979] *A JD is acyclic iff it is equivalent to a set of MVDs.*   □

Thus, an acyclic JD $\bowtie \{X_1, \ldots, X_p\}$ is equivalent to a set of at most $p - 1$ MVDs.

Considering the implication problem $\Sigma \models \sigma$, the chase has been shown to be a decision procedure for FDs and JDs Maier et al. [1979]. This result has been extended to full TGDs and EGDs by Beeri and Vardi [1984]. Moreover, it has been shown that the implication problem is decidable for inclusion dependencies (actually it is PSPACE-complete), but is undecidable for functional and inclusion dependencies Casanova et al. [1984].

Checking lossless decompositions.   Consider a relation schema $(R(U), \Sigma)$, where Σ is a set of FDs and JDs, and let $\Delta = \{U_1, ..., U_n\}$ be a decomposition. To check whether Δ is a lossless-join decomposition it is sufficient to check whether the join dependency $\sigma = \bowtie \{U_1, ..., U_n\}$ is implied by Σ.

Chasing with general data dependencies.   Although the chase has been originally proposed to tackle the implication problem for functional and join dependencies, it can be also used to test implication of more general dependencies, such as TGDs and EGDs. More specifically, if the dependency to be proven is a TGD of the form $\sigma : \forall \mathbf{x} \, \forall \mathbf{z} \, \phi(\mathbf{x}, \mathbf{z}) \rightarrow \exists \mathbf{y} \, \psi(\mathbf{x}, \mathbf{y})$, or an EGD $\sigma : \forall \mathbf{x} \, \phi(\mathbf{x}) \rightarrow (x_1 = x_2)$, the chase procedure consider a set of tableau (instead of a single one) to cover all predicates appearing in the formula. Then, it repeatedly applies the dependencies of Σ by using the chase procedure. It holds that $\Sigma \models \sigma$ if there exists a homomorphism h s.t. $h(\psi(\mathbf{x}, \mathbf{y})) \subseteq chase(\Sigma, \phi(\mathbf{x}, \mathbf{z}))$ (if σ is a TGD), or $(x_1 = x_2)$ is true in $chase(\Sigma, \phi(\mathbf{x}))$ (if σ is an EGD).

Example 6.30   Consider the set of dependencies Σ below:

$$\forall x \, \forall y \, P(x, y) \rightarrow Q(x, y)$$
$$\forall x \, \forall y \, Q(x, y) \rightarrow R(x, y)$$

and the TGD $\sigma = \forall x \, \forall y \, P(x, y) \rightarrow R(x, y)$. To check $\Sigma \models \sigma$, a database D with the three tableau $P = \{(x, y)\}$, $Q = \{\}$ and $R = \{\}$ is built. By chasing D with Σ, we obtain a database containing the tableau $P = \{(x, y)\}$, $Q = \{(x, y)\}$ and $R = \{(x, y)\}$. As $h(R(x, y)) \in chase(\Sigma, D)$, with $h = \{\}$, then $\Sigma \models \sigma$.

Consider the following set of dependencies Σ':

$$\forall x \, \forall y \, P(x, y) \land P(x, z) \rightarrow y = z$$
$$\forall x \, \forall y \, Q(x, y) \land Q(x, z) \rightarrow y = z$$
$$\forall x \, \forall y \, P(x, y) \rightarrow \exists z \, Q(y, z),$$

and the EGD $\sigma' = \forall x \, \forall u \, \forall y \, \forall v \, \forall z \, P(x, u) \land Q(u, y) \land P(x, v) \land Q(v, z) \rightarrow y = z$. To check $\Sigma' \models \sigma'$, a database D' with the two tableau $P = \{(x, u), (u, y)\}$ and $Q = \{(x, v), (v, z)\}$ is built. By chasing D' with Σ' we obtain a database consisting of the relations $P = \{(x, u)\}$ and $Q = \{(u, y)\}$. As we have derived $y = z$, $\Sigma' \models \sigma'$ holds.   □

BIBLIOGRAPHIC NOTES

The study of data dependencies and normal forms was studied intensively in the 1970s and early 1980s in the context of database design. The field started with the introduction of functional dependencies by Codd [1972]. The Boyce-Codd normal form was introduced by Codd [1974]. Multivalued dependencies have been proposed independently by Fagin [1977b] and Zaniolo [1976]. The complete axiomatization for FDs and MVDs has been done by Beeri et al. [1977]. The fourth normal form has been proposed by Fagin [1977a]. Join dependencies have been introduced in full generality by Rissanen [1977]. The FJ/NF has been proposed by Fagin [1979]. Concerning normal forms recently proposed, superkey normal forms were introduced by Normann [1998], the key complete normal form was proposed by Vincent [1997], and the essential tuple normal form was defined by Darwen et al. [2012]. The dependency implication problem was studied by Aho et al. [1979a], who considered the problem of checking whether a set of FDs implies an ID, Maier et al. [1979] and Beeri et al. [1981], who addressed the implication problem using tableau and the chase algorithm, and Beeri and Vardi [1984], who extended the proof to general EGDs and TGDs.

An excellent reference, although not updated, for issues relating to data dependency and normalization theory is [Maier, 1983].

CHAPTER 7

Universal Repairs

In the presence of inconsistencies, the aim of the chase algorithm is to make the database consistent by adding tuples and setting null values. In such a context, it can be assumed that the input database is sound and that inconsistencies are due to missing tuples. However, in some cases, the assumption that the input database is sound is not feasible and the chase algorithm could fail.

Intuitively, a repair of an inconsistent database I is a consistent database J that differs from I in a "minimal" way. The consistent answers to a query Q on an inconsistent database I are the tuples $\bigcap \{Q(J) \mid J \text{ is repair of } I\}$. Therefore, the consistent answers are obtained by considering all repairs and returning the tuples that are guaranteed to be in the result of the query on every repair.

Different types of repairs have been considered in the literature. They can be classified into two different classes: tuple-based repairs, obtained by performing insertion and deletion of tuples [Arenas et al., 1999], and value-based repairs, obtained by performing updates of attribute values [Bertossi et al., 2008, Wijsen, 2005].

In the following, we restrict our attention to tuple-based repairs. Concerning tuple-based repairs, depending on the kind of operation allowed to restore consistency (namely tuple deletions, insertions, or both), three different kinds of repairs are considered: subset-repairs, superset-repairs, and symmetric-difference-repairs. The problem of repairing inconsistent databases and computing consistent answers has been extensively studied in the last years [Afrati and Kolaitis, 2009, Arenas et al., 1999, Caroprese et al., 2009, Chomicki and Marcinkowski, 2005, Flesca et al., 2010, Grahne and Onet, 2010, Greco et al., 2003, Greco and Molinaro, 2012, Lopatenko and Bertossi, 2007, Molinaro and Greco, 2010, Wijsen, 2005]. In the rest of this chapter we concentrate on a particular class of repairs which have a tight connection with the chase. The problem of computing consistent answers over inconsistent databases has also been studied by Fuxman and Miller [2007] and by Wijsen [2010], where consistent answers to queries are computed by rewriting the original query. For a large perspective on querying and repairing inconsistent databases we refer the reader to the excellent book by Bertossi [2011] (see also the survey papers by Bertossi [2006] and Chomicki [2007]).

7.1 UNIVERSAL REPAIRS

When a database is inconsistent, consistency can be restored by inserting and deleting tuples (or, alternatively, updating attribute values) in a "minimal" way, so that the derived database is as close as possible to the original one. The following example illustrates a simple scenario where inconsistency arises.

Example 7.1   Consider the following database containing information regarding football teams.

FTname	Stadium
Real Madrid	Bernabeu
Real Madrid	Calderon
Atletico Madrid	Calderon

Team

Sname	City
Berbabeu	Madrid
Calderon	Madrid

Stadium

Assuming the key dependencies $FTname \rightarrow Stadium$ and $Sname \rightarrow City$, and a foreign key dependency $Team[Stadium] \subseteq Stadium[Sname]$. The database is inconsistent as there are different tuples in the *Team* relation with the same key. In such a case, the chase algorithm fails, but the database could be repaired by deleting one of the two conflicting tuples in the relation *Team*. Tuple-based repairs can be obtained by deleting either the tuple (*Real Madrid, Bernabeu*) or the tuple (*Real Madrid, Calderon*); value-based repairs can be obtained, for instance, by either replacing the value "*Bernabeu*" with "*Calderon*" in the tuple (*Real Madrid, Bernabeu*), or replacing the value "*Calderon*" with "*Bernabeu*" in the tuple (*Real Madrid, Calderon*).   □

Intuitively, a repair of a possibly inconsistent database (with respect to a set of data dependencies) is a consistent database that is as close as possible to the original one.

Definition 7.2 (Repairs)   Let I, J be two databases, and Σ a set of dependencies. We say that J is an $\oplus$-repair of I with respect to Σ if $J \models \Sigma$, and there is no database K such that $K \models \Sigma$ and $I \oplus K \subsetneq I \oplus J$. Here, $\oplus$ denotes the symmetric difference operator. If, in addition, $J \subseteq I$ or $I \subseteq J$, then J is called, respectively, a subset-repair ($\subseteq$-repair) or superset-repair ($\supseteq$-repair).   □

Thus, repairs are consistent databases that are derived from the source database by means of a minimal (under set inclusion) set of tuple insertions and deletions. The set of c-repairs for (I, Σ) will be denoted by $Rep_c(I, \Sigma)$, where $c \in \{\oplus, \subseteq, \supseteq\}$.

Example 7.3   Assume we are given a database $D = \{P(a), P(b), Q(a), Q(c)\}$ with the *inclusion dependency* $\forall x \, P(x) \rightarrow Q(x)$. D is inconsistent since $P(b) \rightarrow Q(b)$ is not satisfied. The repairs for D are $D_1 = \{P(a), P(b), Q(a), Q(c), Q(b)\}$ and $D_2 = \{P(a), Q(a), Q(c)\}$. Observe that D_1 is a $\supseteq$-repair, whereas D_2 is a $\subseteq$-repair.   □

In the presence of databases possibly violating the dependencies defined over their schemas, a widely accepted semantics of query answering is the one based on the notion of consistent answer, which is introduced in the following definition.

Definition 7.4 (Consistent Answer)   Let Σ be a set of dependencies, Q a query, D a database, and $c \in \{\oplus, \subseteq, \supseteq\}$. The c-consistent answers to Q on D with respect to Σ are

$$Con_c(Q, D, \Sigma) = \bigcap\{Q(J)|J \in Rep_c(D, \Sigma)\} .$$

□

It is worth noting that the set of repairs could be infinite for databases with dependencies having existentially quantified variables. In the presence of full dependencies, even if the number of repairs is finite, there can be exponentially many repairs (with respect to the size of the input database).

Example 7.5   Consider the relation schema $R(A, B)$ with the FD $A \rightarrow B$. The relation $r = \{(a_i, b_i), (a_i, c_i) \mid 1 \leq i \leq m\}$ is inconsistent as each A-value a_i is associated with two different B-values b_i and c_i. For such a relation having $2m$ tuples, there are 2^m repairs, and each repair has m tuples.   □

The complexity of computing repairs for different classes of dependencies has been deeply analyzed by Afrati and Kolaitis [2009]. The following table, based on the one presented by Chomicki [2007], recalls most of the data complexity [Vardi, 1984] results of consistent query answering [Arenas et al., 1999, Cali et al., 2003, Chomicki and Marcinkowski, 2005, Greco et al., 2003, Staworko and Chomicki, 2010, Wijsen, 2010]. By *terminating dependencies* we mean the class containing sets of dependencies which are recognized as terminating, independently from the database instance, by some criterion or technique, as previously discussed in Chapter 5.

	Primary keys	Arbitrary keys	Terminating dep.		General dep.	
	$\subseteq$	$\subseteq$	$\supseteq$	$\subseteq, \oplus$	$\subseteq$	$\oplus, \supseteq$
$\sigma, \times, -$	P	P	P	Π_2^p-C	Π_2^p-C	Undec.
$\sigma, \times, -, \cup$	P	P	P	Π_2^p-C	Π_2^p-C	Undec.
σ, π	P	coNP-C	P	Π_2^p-C	Π_2^p-C	Undec.
$\sigma, \pi, \times$	coNP-C	coNP-C	P	Π_2^p-C	Π_2^p-C	Undec.
$\sigma, \pi, \times, -, \cup$	coNP-C	coNP-C	P	Π_2^p-C	Π_2^p-C	Undec.

In the table above, each row refers to a class of queries (specified in terms of the allowed relational algebra operators), while each column refers to a repair semantics and a class of data dependencies (primary keys, arbitrary key dependencies, dependencies for which the chase terminates, general data dependencies). coNP-C and Π_2^p-C stand for coNP-complete and Π_2^p-complete, respectively. For general (existentially quantified) dependencies we have different results depending on the considered repair semantics: for every query class, the problem is undecidable for $\oplus$- and $\supseteq$-repairs, while it is Π_2^p-complete for $\subseteq$-repairs.

Undecidability of computing $\supseteq$-consistent answers for general, existentially quantified dependencies, derives from the fact that in such a case repairs include universal solutions. As the problem of deciding whether the chase fixpoint terminates is, in the general case, undecidable, the problem of deciding whether a set of constraints admit universal solutions, independently from the current database, is undecidable as well. Regarding $\oplus$-consistent answers, the set of universal $\oplus$-repairs includes the universal $\supseteq$-repairs; therefore the problem is undecidable as well.

Such complexity results define upper bounds for general dependencies. As shown in the table, for restricted classes of dependencies the problem is decidable and, in some cases, even tractable. For terminating dependencies the problem is Π_2^p-complete for $\subseteq$- and $\oplus$-repairs, whereas it is in P if $\supseteq$-repairs are considered. Since key dependencies are defined by means of EGDs, databases with (primary) key dependencies do not admit $\supseteq$-repairs. Therefore, for (primary) key dependencies we only consider $\subseteq$-repairs. Complexity results for $\subseteq$-repairs in the presence of primary and arbitrary keys are reported in the first two columns; these results show that, for arbitrary key dependencies, the complexity increases when projection is used.

Further classes of dependencies for which computing consistent answers to conjunctive queries is polynomial time have been identified by Fuxman and Miller [2007] and Wijsen [2010]. These classes allow conjunctive queries to be rewritten into equivalent queries so that it is not necessary to compute repairs, since rewritten queries can be evaluated on the original database and return the consistent answers. As queries are rewritten as FO formulas, the complexity of computing query answers is in AC_0.

By analogy to the notion of a universal solution, universal repairs have recently been introduced [ten Cate et al., 2012].

Definition 7.6   (Universal Repair)   Given a set Σ of dependencies and a database I, a *universal c*-repair (with $c \in \{\oplus, \subseteq, \supseteq\}$) of I with respect to Σ is a *c*-repair J of I with respect to Σ such that, if Q is a conjunctive query, then $Con_c(Q, I, \Sigma) = Q(J)_\downarrow$, where $Q(J)_\downarrow$ is the set of tuples in $Q(J)$ containing only values from the active domain of I.   □

The set of universal *c*-repairs for a database D and set of dependencies Σ will be denoted by $URep_c(D, \Sigma)$, with $c \in \{\oplus, \subseteq, \supseteq\}$.

Example 7.7   Consider the database $D = \{P(a), Q(a)\}$ and the dependency

$$\forall x \; P(x) \wedge Q(x) \rightarrow R(x) \,.$$

There are three $\oplus$-repairs: $D_1 = \{P(a)\}$, $D_2 = \{Q(a)\}$, and $D_3 = \{P(a), Q(a), R(a)\}$. D_1 and D_2 are $\subseteq$-repairs, whereas D_3 is a $\supseteq$-repair. As D_3 is the unique $\supseteq$-repair, it is also universal. Regarding the $\subseteq$-repairs, both D_1 and D_2 are not universal.   □

It is worth noting that for any database I and set of dependencies Σ: (i) there is at most one universal $\supseteq$-repair, up to isomorphism, which can be computed using the chase fixpoint algorithm; and (ii) there is at most one universal $\subseteq$-repair which coincides with the unique $\subseteq$-repair, if such a unique repair exists. Consequently, if I and Σ admit more than one $\subseteq$-repair, then there is no universal $\subseteq$-repair.

Moreover, the presence of EGDs limits the existence of universal repairs. Consider, for instance, a database I and an EGD $\sigma = \forall \mathbf{x} \phi(\mathbf{x}) \rightarrow x_1 = x_2$. If $I \not\models \sigma$ and x_1 and x_2 appear in different body atoms in $\phi(\mathbf{x})$, then there are neither universal $\subseteq$-repairs nor universal $\supseteq$-repairs. Regarding $\oplus$-repairs, we have that if I and Σ have a universal $\oplus$-repair, then it is a universal $\subseteq$-repair as well. Moreover, as shown by the following example, it is possible to have universal $\subseteq$-repairs which are not universal $\oplus$-repairs.

Example 7.8   Consider the database $I = \{P(a), Q(a)\}$ and the following set of TGDs Σ:

$$\forall x \, [P(x) \rightarrow \exists y \, Q(y)]$$
$$\forall x \, [P(x) \wedge Q(x) \rightarrow R(x)] \quad .$$

$J = \{Q(a)\}$ is the unique (universal) $\subseteq$-repair, but is not a universal $\oplus$-repair as even the simple query consisting of the single atom $Q(x)$ does not return the consistent answers when evaluated on J. In fact, the query returns the tuple (a) when evaluated on J, but this is not a consistent answer as it cannot be derived from $K_1 = \{P(a) \wedge Q(b)\}$ which is also an $\oplus$-repair. $\square$

7.2   SPECIAL CLASSES OF DEPENDENCIES

Special classes of dependencies guarantee the existence of universal repairs. In this section we consider LAV and GAV dependencies and report some results for them.

   A *local-as-view* (LAV) TGD is a TGD

$$\forall \mathbf{x} \, R(\mathbf{x}) \rightarrow \exists \mathbf{y} \, \psi(\mathbf{x}, \mathbf{y})$$

where the body is a single atom. A *global-as-view* (GAV) TGD is a full TGD

$$\forall \mathbf{x} \, \forall \mathbf{y} \, \phi(\mathbf{x}, \mathbf{y}) \rightarrow R(\mathbf{x})$$

where the head is a single atom.

Example 7.9   The dependency

$$\forall x \, \forall y \, F(x, y) \rightarrow \exists z \, E(x, z) \wedge E(z, y)$$

is a LAV TGD, whereas the dependency

$$\forall x \, \forall z \, \forall y \, E(x, z) \wedge E(z, y) \rightarrow F(x, y)$$

is a GAV TGD. The dependency

$$\forall x \, \forall y \, E(x, y) \rightarrow F(x, y)$$

is both LAV and GAV. $\square$

A set of dependencies Σ is *closed under union* (resp. *closed under intersection*) if, for all pair of databases I and J such that $I \models \Sigma$ and $J \models \Sigma$ it holds, $I \cup J \models \Sigma$ (resp. $I \cap J \models \Sigma$).

It turns out that dependencies closed under union guarantee the existence of universal $\oplus$- and $\subseteq$-repairs (we will discuss properties for dependencies closed under intersection in the following, when GAV dependencies are discussed in more detail).

Proposition 7.10   *Let Σ be a set of dependencies. The following statements are equivalent.*

1. *Σ is closed under union.*

2. *Every database has a universal $\oplus$-repair w.r.t. Σ.*

3. *Every database has a universal $\subseteq$-repair w.r.t. Σ.*   □

7.2.1   LAV

LAV dependencies enjoy nice properties in terms of existence of universal repairs and efficient computation of answers to conjunctive queries. The following theorem states that: (i) LAV dependencies are closed under union, and (ii) terminating TGDs that are closed under union are equivalent to a set of LAV dependencies. Thus, in such settings the existence of universal $\oplus$- and $\subseteq$-repairs is guaranteed.

Theorem 7.11   *For every set of TGDs Σ:*

- *if Σ is a LAV TGDs, then it is closed under union;*

- *if Σ is terminating and closed under union, then there exists a set of LAV TGDs that is equivalent to Σ.*   □

Furthermore, when the set of dependencies consists of LAV TGDs, there exists a unique universal $\subseteq$-repair and a unique universal $\oplus$-repair, and they coincide.

Clearly, if Σ is a set of LAV TGDs, then every database I has a unique $\subseteq$-repair, which is also the unique universal $\subseteq$-repair and the unique universal $\oplus$-repair of I w.r.t. Σ. The following theorem states that, in the presence of LAV TGDs, the universal $\subseteq$-repair (which coincides with the universal $\oplus$-repair) exists and can be computed in polynomial time. Furthermore, for any $c \in \{\oplus, \subseteq, \supseteq\}$, both the c-consistent query answering decision problem with conjunctive queries and the c-repair checking problem can be solved in polynomial time.

Theorem 7.12   [ten Cate et al., 2012] *Let Σ be a set of LAV TGDs. Then we have the following.*

- *For any $c \in \{\oplus, \subseteq, \supseteq\}$, the c-repair checking problem with respect to Σ is solvable in polynomial time.*

- *There is a polynomial-time algorithm that, given a database I, computes the unique universal $\subseteq$-repair of I with respect to Σ (which is also the unique universal $\oplus$-repair of I with respect to Σ).*

- *For every conjunctive query Q, and for $c \in \{\oplus, \subseteq, \supseteq\}$, the c-consistent query answering problem with respect to Σ is solvable in polynomial time.* □

7.2.2 GAV

For GAV dependencies we would expect "dual" characterizations with respect to LAV dependencies. First of all, it is worth noting that GAV dependencies are universally quantified and, therefore, termination of the chase fixpoint is guaranteed. As shown by the following example, GAV TGDs are not closed under union.

Example 7.13 Consider the databases $I = \{P(a)\}$ and $J = \{Q(a)\}$, and the GAV TGD

$$\sigma = \forall x \; P(x) \wedge Q(x) \rightarrow R(x) \, .$$

Both databases are consistent as $I \models \sigma$ and $J \models \Sigma$, but $I \cup J \not\models \sigma$. □

Moreover, considering the previous example, we have that $I \cap J \models \sigma$. Indeed, GAV TGDs are closed under intersection, and it turns out that dependencies closed under intersection guarantee the existence of universal $\supseteq$-repairs.

Theorem 7.14 *Let Σ be a set of TGDs. Then, the following statements are equivalent.*

1. *Every database has a unique (universal) $\supseteq$-repair with respect to Σ.*

2. *Σ is closed under intersection.*

3. *Σ is logically equivalent to a set of GAV TGDs.* □

Thus, when GAV TGDs are considered, there is a unique (universal) $\supseteq$-repair. Furthermore, it can be computed in polynomial time.

Theorem 7.15 *Let Σ be a set of GAV TGDs. Given a database I, there is an algorithm, running in polynomial time in the size of I, that computes the unique (universal) $\supseteq$-repair of I with respect to Σ.* □

It follows from the previous theorem that the $\supseteq$-consistent query answering problem can be solved in polynomial in the presence of GAV TGDs. Unfortunately, this does not hold anymore if we consider the $\subset$- and $\oplus$-consistent query answering problems.

Theorem 7.16 [ten Cate et al., 2012] *There is a set Σ consisting of a single GAV TGD and a conjunctive query Q, such that both the $\subseteq$-consistent query answering problem and the $\oplus$-consistent query answering problem for Q with respect to Σ are CoNP-complete.* □

7.2.3   TERMINATING DEPENDENCIES

The result stating that GAV TGDs have a unique (universal) $\supseteq$-repair can be generalized to the whole class of full TGDs. An important class of TGDs with nice properties, that further extends the class of full TGDs, is that of terminating TGDs. That is, the class of TGDs for which chase termination is guaranteed, according to the criteria of Chapter 5. Indeed, in such a setting, it is possible to check in polynomial time whether a $\supseteq$-repair exists and, if it exists, to compute in polynomial time the unique (up to isomorphism) universal $\supseteq$-repair.

It is worth noting that, for every terminating set of TGDs and EGDs Σ, and for every database I, if there is a $\supseteq$-repair J for I with respect to Σ, then J is a universal $\supseteq$-repair. Since such a $\supseteq$-repair can be computed using the chase algorithm, there is a polynomial time algorithm that checks whether I has a $\supseteq$-repair with respect to Σ. And if so, computes the (unique up to isomorphism) universal $\supseteq$-repair of I. The size of the computed repair is polynomial in the size of the source database.

In such a scenario, the size of any $\oplus$-repair is also polynomially bounded by the size of the original database. With EGDs and a terminating set of TGDs, the consistent query answering problem is in PTIME if we consider $\supseteq$-repairs, but it becomes Π_2^p-complete if $\oplus$- or $\subseteq$-repairs are considered. The following theorem, which in its original formulation was stated for acyclic dependencies, introduces upper bounds for the conjunctive query answering problem.

Theorem 7.17   [ten Cate et al., 2012] *Let Σ be a terminating set of TGDs and EGDs, and let Q be a conjunctive query.*

1. *The $\supseteq$-consistent query answering problem for Q with respect to Σ is in PTIME.*

2. *The $\oplus$-consistent (resp. subset-consistent) query answering problem for Q with respect to Σ is in Π_2^p.*

3. *There is a set Σ of weakly acyclic TGDs and a conjunctive query Q, such that both the $\oplus$-consistent and the $\subseteq$-consistent query answering problems for q with respect to Σ are Π_2^p-complete.* $\square$

BIBLIOGRAPHIC NOTES

The first notion of repair, based on a minimal (under set inclusion) set of changes, was introduced by Arenas et al. [1999]. Next, several different variations of repairs were proposed based on different minimality criteria. For instance, minimal cardinality repairs were proposed by Lopatenko and Bertossi [2007], whereas repairs with three-valued semantics (where databases contain both true and uncertain information) were studied by Furfaro et al. [2007].

Attribute-based repairs, that is repairs obtained by changing some attribute values in existing tuples, were studied by Wijsen [2005] and Bohannon et al. [2005]. Attribute-based repairs minimizing a numerical aggregation function over the attribute-value changes were proposed by Flesca et al. [2010] and Bertossi et al. [2008].

Consistent query answering and repairs have also been considered in other contexts such as XML databases [Flesca et al., 2003, Staworko and Chomicki, 2006], multi-dimensional databases [Yaghmaie et al., 2012], and spatial databases [Rodríguez et al., 2008, 2011]. Probabilistic representation of repairs and probabilistic answers were studied by Andritsos et al. [2006] and by Greco and Molinaro [2012].

Techniques for computing answers based on the rewriting of source queries were studied by [Arenas et al., 1999, Fuxman and Miller, 2007, Wijsen, 2010]. The complexity of computing repairs was analyzed by Afrati and Kolaitis [2009]. Universal repairs were introduced by ten Cate et al. [2012]. Surveys of the area were published by Bertossi [2006] and Chomicki [2007]. The monograph Bertossi [2011] is an updated overview of the field.

CHAPTER 8

Chase and Database Applications

This chapter describes several database applications in which some typical database problems arise, and where the chase represents a fundamental tool for their solution. In every case, the termination of the chase algorithm guarantees the applicability of the proposed resolution methods.

Although the chase has been originally proposed to tackle the implication problem for data dependencies, it has been also used in several other contexts, such as checking *query containment under constraints* and *query optimization*. More recently, the chase procedure has gained a lot of attention due to its usefulness in *data integration* [Cali et al., 2004, Lenzerini, 2002], *ontology-based* data management [Cali et al., 2009a,b], *inconsistent databases* and *data repairs* [Afrati and Kolaitis, 2009, Arenas et al., 1999] (see also Chapter 7), *data exchange* [Fagin et al., 2005a], *peer data exchange* [Fuxman et al., 2005], and *data correspondence* [Grahne and Onet, 2010].

In this chapter we deal with the role of the chase in query containment and optimization, and we review two important database applications, namely data integration and data exchange, where both problems make use of the chase procedure in the process of finding solutions. Finally, we describe the problem of *querying answering on incomplete data*, that we find both in data exchange and data integration, and show solutions proposed for conjunctive queries and non-monotonic queries.

8.1 QUERY CONTAINMENT UNDER CONSTRAINTS

Query containment under constraints is the problem of checking whether, for every database satisfying a given set of constraints, the result of a query is a subset of the result of another query. Containment of queries over relational databases has long been considered a fundamental problem in query optimization, especially query containment under constraints such as TGDs and EGDs.

Definition 8.1 (Query containment) Consider a database schema $\mathbf{R}$ and two queries Q_1 and Q_2 expressed over $\mathbf{R}$. We say that Q_1 is contained in Q_2, denoted as $Q_1 \subseteq Q_2$, if for every database D over $\mathbf{R}$, $Q_1(D)$ is contained in $Q_2(D)$. □

We say that the queries Q_1 and Q_2 are equivalent, denoted $Q_1 \equiv Q_2$, if both $Q_1 \subseteq Q_2$ and $Q_2 \subseteq Q_1$ hold.

The following algorithm tests query containment in the case of conjunctive queries (a Datalog rule is used to express a conjunctive query with $body(Q)$ and $head(Q)$ denoting, respectively, the head and the body of the Datalog query Q). Let Q_1 and Q_2 be two conjunctive queries.

1. Freeze $body(Q_1)$ and $head(Q_1)$ by turning each variable into a distinct (fresh) constant.

2. Evaluate Q_2 over the frozen body of Q_1.

3. $Q_1 \subseteq Q_2$ iff the evaluation returns the frozen head of Q_1.

Example 8.2   Consider the following two conjunctive queries:

$$Q_1 : p(X, Z) \leftarrow a(X, Y) \wedge a(Y, Z)$$

$$Q_2 : p(X, Z) \leftarrow a(X, U) \wedge a(V, Z) .$$

We want to check whether $Q_1 \subseteq Q_2$. Thus, following the algorithm above, we freeze $body(Q_1)$ and $head(Q_1)$ thereby obtaining:

Frozen $body(Q_1)$:

$$a(0, 1) \leftarrow$$

$$a(1, 2) \leftarrow$$

Frozen $head(Q_1)$:

$$p(0, 2) \leftarrow$$

Then, we evaluate Q_2 on the frozen body of Q_1, that is

$$Q_2(\{a(0, 1), a(1, 2)\}) = \{p(0, 2)\}$$

which is exactly the frozen head of Q_1. Thus, we can conclude that $Q_1 \subseteq Q_2$. $\square$

Unfortunately, checking query containment in the presence of constraints becomes more difficult, as it is needed to reason on the constraints imposed by the schema.

Definition 8.3   (Query containment under constraints)   Consider a database schema $\mathbf{R}$, a set Σ of constraints over $\mathbf{R}$, and two queries Q_1 and Q_2 expressed over $\mathbf{R}$. We say that Q_1 is contained in Q_2 under Σ, denoted $Q_1 \subseteq_\Sigma Q_2$, if for every database instance D over $\mathbf{R}$ such that $D \models \Sigma$ it holds $Q_1(D) \subseteq Q_2(D)$. If $Q_1 \subseteq_\Sigma Q_2$ and $Q_2 \subseteq_\Sigma Q_1$, then we say that Q_1 and Q_2 are equivalent under Σ, denoted $Q_1 \equiv_\Sigma Q_2$. $\square$

The following theorem shows that the chase is used to reduce the conjunctive query containment under tuple generating dependencies to classical query containment.

Theorem 8.4   *[Deutsch et al., 2008, Johnson and Klug, 1984] Consider a database schema $\mathbf{R}$, a set Σ of TGDs over $\mathbf{R}$, and two conjunctive queries Q_1, Q_2 expressed over $\mathbf{R}$. Then, $Q_1 \subseteq_\Sigma Q_2$ iff $h(head(Q_1)) \in Q_2(chase(\Sigma, h(body(Q_1))))$, where h is a homomorphism that maps every distinct variable in Q_1 into a distinct fresh constant.* $\square$

The idea is to freeze Q_1 and construct a generic database that provides answers to Q_1; however, as this database must satisfy the set of constraints Σ, we apply the chase to the frozen query body. Observe that in the previous theorem $h(body(Q_1))$ defines a database and the query Q_2 is applied to the database obtained by chasing such a database with Σ.

Example 8.5 Consider the database schema $\mathbf{R} = \{Employee(EmpId, Salary, Dept), Department(DeptId, Location)\}$ along with the following inclusion dependency σ:

$$\forall x_1 \, \forall x_2 \, \forall x_3 \; Employee(x_1, x_2, x_3) \rightarrow \exists y_1 \, \exists y_2 \; Department(x_3, y_1, y_2) \, .$$

Consider now the following two conjunctive queries:

$$Q_1 : P(x) \leftarrow Employee(x, y, z) \wedge Department(z, w)$$
$$Q_2 : P(x) \leftarrow Employee(x, y, z) \, .$$

It is easy to see that $Q_1 \subseteq Q_2$, but $Q_2 \nsubseteq Q_1$. However, we have that $Q_2 \subseteq_{\{\sigma\}} Q_1$. In fact, by considering h s.t. $h(x) = a, h(y) = b$ and $h(z) = c$, we obtain:

$$D = chase(\{\sigma\}, h(body(Q_2))) = \{Employee(a, b, c), Department(b, \eta_1, \eta_2)\}$$

and

$$h(head(Q_1)) = \{P(a)\} \subseteq Q_1(D) = \{P(a)\} \, .$$

If follows that $Q_1 \equiv_{\{\sigma\}} Q_2$. □

Unfortunately, the previous result can be applied only when the chase is terminating for the set of embedded dependencies Σ. To test containment of conjunctive queries under inclusion dependencies alone or *key-based dependencies* (a special class of FDs and IDs that is more general than the combination of key and foreign key dependencies), Johnson and Klug [1984] proved that it is sufficient to consider a *finite* portion of the chase. This leads to the decidability of the query containment problem, although the complexity of the problem is PSPACE-complete [Casanova et al., 1984].

Other decidable classes of dependencies have been studied in the last ten years, in the context of *query answering on incomplete databases*. In fact, query containment and query answering under constraints have been shown to be tightly connected (see Section 8.5), as the implication problem can be reduced to both problems.

8.2 QUERY OPTIMIZATION

The query optimization problem consists in finding a query Q_m equivalent to a given query Q such that Q_m has a lower (possibly minimal) cost with respect to the cost of Q.

The *query reformulation problem* is defined as follows: given a query Q_1 and a set of constraints Σ, decide whether there exists a query Q_2 such that $Q_1 \equiv_\Sigma Q_2$ (cf. Definition 8.3) and the cost of computing Q_2, denoted by $const(Q_2)$, is lower than the cost of computing Q_1. Of course, there may be infinitely many queries Q_2 equivalent to Q_1, and since we want to actually compute a Q_2 when it exists, we choose among all possible Q_2's by using cost criteria. The *query minimization problem* consists in searching for an equivalent query Q_2 that satisfies some syntactically determined minimality condition.

In the case of conjunctive queries and the constraints that are TGDs and EGDs, the *chase and backchase* algorithm has been proposed to solve the query minimization problem [Deutsch et al., 1999, 2006, Popa et al., 2000]. In this case, the adopted *minimality criterion* is the following: a conjunctive query Q is Σ-minimal if there do not exist two queries Q_1 and Q_2 such that Q_1 is obtained from Q by replacing zero or more variables with other variables of Q, Q_2 is obtained from Q_1 by dropping at least one atom from Q_1, and $Q \equiv_\Sigma Q_1 \equiv_\Sigma Q_2$.

The chase and backchase algorithm proceeds in two phases.

1. In the *chase phase*, the original query Q is chased with the constraints in Σ, yielding a query U, called a *universal plan*.

2. Then, the *backchase phase* enumerates all Σ-minimal subqueries SQ of U such that $SQ \equiv_\Sigma Q$.

The backchase phase is so called because it needs to test $SQ \equiv_\Sigma Q$ by checking both $SQ \subseteq_\Sigma Q$ and $SQ \supseteq_\Sigma Q$, using again the chase procedure.

The applicability of the backchase algorithm requires the chase to terminate with the set of constraints Σ.

8.3   DATA EXCHANGE

In data exchange [Fagin et al., 2005a], data structured under one schema (called *source schema*) must be restructured and translated into an instance of a different schema (called *target schema*). Let **S** be the source schema and **T** be the target schema; we assume that **S** and **T** are disjoint. Moreover, since **T** is an independently created schema, it has its own set of constraints, denoted as Σ_t. The mappings relating source and target schema are expressed as *source-to-target TGDs* Σ_{st}, which specify how and what source data should appear in the target. More formally, the *data exchange setting* is defined as follows.

Definition 8.6   A schema mapping (or data exchange setting) is a 4-tuple $M = (\mathbf{S}, \mathbf{T}, \Sigma_{st}, \Sigma_t)$ where:

- **S** is the source schema,

- **T** is the target schema,

- Σ_{st} is a set of source-to-target TGDs of the form $\phi_\mathbf{S}(\mathbf{x}, \mathbf{z}) \rightarrow \exists \mathbf{y}\, \psi_\mathbf{T}(\mathbf{x}, \mathbf{y})$, where $\phi_\mathbf{S}(\mathbf{x}, \mathbf{z})$ is a conjunction of atoms over **S**, $\psi_\mathbf{T}(\mathbf{x}, \mathbf{y})$ is a conjunction of atoms over **T**, and every variable in $\mathbf{x} \cup \mathbf{z}$ occurs in an atom in $\phi_\mathbf{S}(\mathbf{x}, \mathbf{z})$, and,

- Σ_t is a set of target dependencies, where each target dependency in Σ_t is either a TGD $\phi_T(\mathbf{x}, \mathbf{z}) \rightarrow \exists \mathbf{y} \, \psi_T(\mathbf{x}, \mathbf{y})$ or an EGD $\phi_T(\mathbf{x}) \rightarrow (x_1 = x_2)$.   □

Thus, the *data exchange problem* associated with a setting M is the following: Given a database D over $\mathbf{S}$, find a target database J over $\mathbf{T}$ such that $\langle D, J \rangle$ satisfies Σ_{st} and J satisfies Σ_t. J is called a solution for D or simply a solution if D is understood. It is worth noting that the input to a data exchange problem is a database over the source schema only and the data exchange setting (i.e. source and target schemas and dependencies) is considered fixed.

Example 8.7   Consider the data exchange setting $M = (\mathbf{S}, \mathbf{T}, \Sigma_{st}, \Sigma_t)$ described below. The source schema $\mathbf{S}$ has one relation $Dept\,Emp(dpt\_id, mgr\_name, eid)$ listing departments with their managers and their employees. The target schema $\mathbf{T}$ has a relation $Dept(dpt\_id, mgr\_id, mgr\_name)$ for departments and their managers, and a separate relation for employees $Emp(eid, dpt\_id)$. The source-to-target and target dependencies are:

$$\Sigma_{st} = \{Dept\,Emp(d, n, e) \rightarrow \exists w (Dept(d, w, n) \land Emp(e, d))\}$$

$$\Sigma_t = \{Dept(d, m, n) \rightarrow Emp(m, d), \quad Emp(e, d) \rightarrow \exists u \exists v Dept(d, u, v)\}.$$

Suppose the source instance is $D = \{Dept\,Emp(CS, Mary, E003)\}$. A possible solution for D is $J_1 = \{Dept(CS, Mary, Mary), Emp(E003, CS)\}$.   □

Observe that there may be many solutions (or none) for a given instance of the data exchange problem. The set of all solutions is denoted by $Sol(D, \Sigma_{st} \cup \Sigma_t)$. However, a special class of solutions has been identified for the semantics of the data exchange problem, namely the class of *universal solutions* for D. This kind of solution is justified by the fact that a universal solution is representative of the space of all solutions, as it can be mapped into any other solution. The set of all universal solutions for D is denoted by $USol(D, \Sigma_{st} \cup \Sigma_t)$. For instance, for the previous example, a universal solution for D is $J_2 = \{Dept(CS, \eta_1, Mary), Emp(E003, CS), Emp(\eta_1, CS), Dept(CS, \eta_2, \eta_3)\}$.

As we saw in Chapter 4, a universal solution J for D and $\Sigma_{st} \cup \Sigma_t$ can be computed by using the chase algorithm, i.e., $J = chase(\Sigma_{st} \cup \Sigma_t, D)$. In this case, J is called a *canonical universal solution*. Moreover, if $chase(\Sigma_{st} \cup \Sigma_t, D)$ fails, no solution exists for the assigned data exchange problem. For arbitrary sets of target dependencies, there may not exist a finite chase. Thus, the identification of special classes of constraints for which the chase termination is guaranteed in polynomial time data complexity is also relevant in the data exchange context. The identification of these classes has been the object of Chapter 5.

The semantics of target query answering adopts the notion of *certain answers*, i.e., the answers to a query Q are all those tuples t of constants such that, for every solution J of the data exchange problem, $t \in Q(J)$. For the class of union of conjunctive queries it has been shown that computing certain answers to a query Q is equivalent to evaluating Q over a universal solution J, and taking all the tuples of constants in $Q(J)$. This result holds since conjunctive queries are preserved under homomorphisms.

8.4 DATA INTEGRATION

The task of a *data integration system* is to combine data residing at different sources, providing the user with a unified view of them, called *global schema*. User queries are formulated over the global schema, and the system suitably queries the sources providing an answer to the user, who is not obliged to have any information about the sources.

A central aspect of query processing is the specification of the relationship between the global schema and the sources; such a specification is given in the form of a mapping. More formally, using the notation previously used for a schema mapping, the data integration problem can be stated as follows:

Definition 8.8   An *information integration system* is a 4-tuple $\mathcal{I} = (S, G, \Sigma_{SG}, \Sigma_G)$, where S and G are the source and global schemas, Σ_G is a set of integrity constraints over G, and Σ_{SG} is the mapping between S and G.[1]   □

The global schema is a representation of the domain of interest of the data integration system: integrity constraints are expressed on such a schema to enhance its expressiveness, thus improving its capability of representing the real world. Regarding the mapping, there are basically two approaches for specifying it (already discussed in Section 7.2): the *global-as-view* (GAV), requiring that a view over the sources is associated with every relation of the global schema, and the *local-as-view* (LAV), requiring the sources to be defined as views over the global schema (Duschka and Levy [1997], Lenzerini [2002]).

Example 8.9   Consider a global schema with the following relation schemas:

$$movie(Title, Year, Director)$$
$$european(Director)$$
$$review(Title, Critique) \, .$$

The source schema consists of the following three relation schemas:

$$s_1(Title, Year, Director)$$
$$s_2(Title, Critique) \, ,$$

where relation s_1 stores title, year, and director of movies with European director, and relation s_2 stores title and critique of movies.

A GAV mapping associating with each relation name of the global schema a view over the source schema is as follows:

$$\forall x \, \forall y \, \forall z \; s_1(x, y, z) \rightarrow movie(x, y, z)$$
$$\forall x \, \forall y \, \forall z \; s_1(x, y, z) \rightarrow european(z)$$
$$\forall x \, \forall y \; s_2(x, y) \rightarrow review(x, y)$$

---

[1]Traditionally, an information integration system $\mathcal{I}$ is a triple $\langle \mathcal{G}, S, \mathcal{M} \rangle$, where $\mathcal{G} = \langle G, \Sigma_G \rangle$ is the global schema specified by a set of relations G and a set of integrity constraints Σ_G on G, S is the source schema, and $\mathcal{M}$ is the mapping between S and G.

while, a LAV mapping is defined as follows:

$$\forall x\, \forall y\, \forall z\; s_1(x, y, z) \rightarrow movie(x, y, z) \wedge european(z)$$
$$\forall x\, \forall y\; s_2(x, y) \rightarrow \exists u\, \exists v\; movie(x, u, v) \wedge review(x, y)\,.$$

$\square$

Sources are in general autonomous and the data that they provide are likely not to satisfy the constraints on the global schema. For this reason, the integrity constraints Σ_G have to be taken into account during query processing; otherwise, the system may return incorrect answers to the user [Bravo and Bertossi, 2003, Cali et al., 2004, Fagin et al., 2005a].

Another significant issue is that the sources may not provide exactly the data that satisfy the corresponding portion of the global schema; in particular, they may provide either a subset or a superset of the data satisfying the mentioned portion, and the mapping is to be considered *sound* or *complete*, respectively. Mappings that are both sound and complete are called *exact*.

The semantics for a data integration system $\mathcal{I}$ is the set of all databases that satisfy $\mathcal{I}$, i.e., the logical models of $\Sigma_{SG} \cup \Sigma_G$. Given a source database D over the source schema S (called a *source database* for $\mathcal{I}$), the set of all databases over G that satisfy $\mathcal{I}$ relative to D is denoted as $sem_x(\mathcal{I}, D) = sem_x(\Sigma_{SG} \cup \Sigma_G, D)$, where $x \in \{s, c, e\}$ (for sound, complete, and exact semantics, respectively).

Let $\{I\} = Rep_{\supseteq}(D, \Sigma_{SG})$, $sem_x(\Sigma_{SG} \cup \Sigma_G, D)$ for sound, complete, and exact semantics, is defined as follows:

1. $sem_s(\Sigma_{SG} \cup \Sigma_G, D) = Rep_{\supseteq}(I, \Sigma_G)$;

2. $sem_c(\Sigma_{SG} \cup \Sigma_G, D) = Rep_{\subseteq}(I, \Sigma_G)$;

3. $sem_e(\Sigma_{SG} \cup \Sigma_G, D) = \{I \mid I \models \Sigma_G\}$.

This means that $sem_s(\Sigma_{SG} \cup \Sigma_G, D)$ (resp. $sem_c(\Sigma_{SG} \cup \Sigma_G, D)$, $sem_e(\Sigma_{SG} \cup \Sigma_G, D)$) consists of all databases J such that (i) $\langle D, J \rangle \models \Sigma_{SG}$, (ii) $J \models \Sigma_G$ and (iii) $I \subseteq J$ (resp. $I \supseteq J$, $I = J$).

The semantics of query answering is the following. Given a source database D for $\mathcal{I}$ we call *answers* to a query Q of arity n w.r.t. $\mathcal{I}$ and D, the set $Q(D, \mathcal{I})$ defined as follows: $Q(D, \mathcal{I}) = \{\langle c_1, \ldots, c_n \rangle \mid for\ each\ B \in sem_x(\mathcal{I}, D), \langle c_1, \ldots, c_n \rangle \in Q(B)\}$.

Dealing with Incomplete Data

The problem of query answering in the presence of incomplete data also arises in data integration scenarios. Query processing in LAV (without global constraints) was traditionally considered a form of reasoning in the presence of incomplete information. In fact, sources in LAV data integration systems are generally assumed to be sound, but not necessarily complete (each view is assumed to store only a subset of the data that satisfy the corresponding view on the global schema). Query answering in LAV with global constraints was considered in Bertossi and Bravo [2005], Bravo and Bertossi [2003].

Query processing in GAV (without global constraints), instead, is less involved as the form of the mapping straightforwardly allows for the computation of a global database instance, i.e., the *retrieved global database* $ret(\mathcal{I}, D) = chase(\Sigma_{SG}, D)$, over which the query can be directly evaluated. It is worth noting that this approach is analogous to *unfolding* queries with respect to the mapping, i.e., substitute each atom in the query with its correspondent view specified by the mapping, and evaluating the unfolded queries directly on the source database. In this case, the views over the source relations defined by the mappings are trivially exact, as $\Sigma_G = \emptyset$. However, in GAV it may also happen that the sources are considered sound rather than exact, in particular when integrity constraints are specified on the global schema. In this case, the query unfolding is no more sufficient, and reasoning by taking constraints into account is needed in order to compute the certain answers to a query. Moreover, it is easy to see that reasoning about the constraints is also needed in the LAV approach.

8.5 QUERY ANSWERING ON INCOMPLETE DATA

In this section we deal with the problem of conjunctive query answering on incomplete databases, where integrity constraints are TGDs and EGDs. In addition, we also assume that the database is sound, i.e., it satisfies the EGDs specified by the schema (this means that the chase cannot fail). In this case, if the TGDs are not satisfied, we may add suitable facts to the database in order to satisfy them (according to the sound semantics we cannot delete facts from the database to solve such violations). Of course, the new tuples added to the database must be consistent with respect to the EGDs.

The (decisional) problem of conjunctive query answering on incomplete data is the following: Given a relational schema $\mathbf{R}$, a set Σ of TGDs and EGDs over $\mathbf{R}$, a database instance D that may not satisfy the constraints in Σ, a conjunctive query Q, and a tuple t, is t an answer to Q in every database instance $B \in sem_s(\Sigma, D)$ (cf. Section 8.4)?

The set of all tuples t such that $t \in Q(B)$ for every $B \in sem_s(\Sigma, D)$ is denoted as $Q(D, \Sigma)$.

Theorem 8.10   *[Deutsch et al., 2008] Consider a relation schema $\mathbf{R}$, a set Σ of TGDs over $\mathbf{R}$, and an atom t; we have that $t \in Q(D, \Sigma)$ iff $chase(\Sigma, D) \models t$.* $\square$

This result holds because the (possibly infinite) chase is a universal solution and then a representative of all the databases in $sem_s(\Sigma, D)$. The following well-known result show the tight connection between conjunctive query containment and conjunctive query answering in incomplete data.

Theorem 8.11   *[Cali et al., 2008] Under TGDs, the (decisional) problem of conjunctive query answering on incomplete data and the problem of conjunctive query containment are mutually PTIME-reducible.* $\square$

It is worth noting that, even if the chase in Theorem 8.10 may be infinite, $chase(\Sigma, D) \models t$ remains well defined. However, we do not have query evaluation on an infinite instance.

In this scenario, conditions guaranteeing the termination of the chase algorithm over a set of TGDs for all database instances become a useful tool to allow query answering on incomplete databases. Recently, very interesting results have been exhibited for classes of TGDs for which the problem is decidable even if the chase does not halt.

Example 8.12 Consider the following TGD

$$\sigma : R(x, y) \rightarrow \exists z\, R(y, z)$$

and the database instance $D = \{R(a, b)\}$. Clearly, there is no universal solution for D and σ, as the TGD can be applied an infinite number of times. In particular, we have that $chase(\{\sigma\}, D) = \{R(a, b), R(b, \eta_1), R(\eta_1, \eta_2), R(\eta_2, \eta_3), \dots\}$.

Consider now the query $q(x) \leftarrow R(x, y)$. Even if the universal solution is infinite, it is easy to see that the certain answers to the query contain the tuples $\{(a), (b)\}$. □

However, when dependencies belong to one of the following cases, it is sufficient to consider only a finite portion of the chase, depending on the query, in order to answer to union of conjunctive queries [Cali et al., 2003, 2008, 2009a, 2010]:

- inclusion dependencies;

- *guarded TGDs*, that is TGDs characterized by the presence of a *guard*, namely an atom in the body that contains all the (universally quantified) variables in the TGD body;

- *weakly guarded TGDs*, that are characterized by the presence of a *weak guard* containing all the (universally quantified) variables in the TGD body appearing in affected positions;

- *linear TGDs*, that is TGDs having exactly one atom in the body and one atom in the head; they are the closest class to inclusion dependencies, and they correspond to inclusion dependencies with repetition of columns;

- *sticky sets of TGDs*, which are sets of TGDs with a restriction on multiple occurrences of variables (including joins) in the TGD bodies.

Adding equality generating dependencies to the constraints may in general lead to undecidability of query answering, in fact the problem is undecidable already for inclusion dependencies and key dependencies [Cali et al., 2003]. However, in order to deal with EGDs, the notion of *separability* was proposed by Cali et al. [2003].

Definition 8.13 (Separability) Consider a set Σ_T of TGDs over a schema $\mathbf{R}$, and a set Σ_E of EGDs over $\mathbf{R}$. We say that the set $\Sigma = \Sigma_T \cup \Sigma_E$ is *separable* if, for every database D over $\mathbf{R}$, either (i) $chase(\Sigma, D)$ fails or (ii) $chase(\Sigma, D) \models Q$ iff $chase(\Sigma_T, D) \models Q$ for every boolean conjunctive query Q over $\mathbf{R}$. □

In other words, separability holds if, when there exists at least one solution for Σ and D, the presence of EGDs does not change query answering. It follows that, if the property of separability holds, queries can be answered by considering the TGDs only (apart from an initial check whether the chase fails). Some examples of separable classes of TGDs and EGDs are *non-key-conflicting (NKC) IDs* [Cali et al., 2003] and *non-key-conflicting TGDs* [Cali et al., 2009a]. Further classes were defined in [Cali and Pieris, 2011, Cali et al., 2010].

BEYOND CONJUNCTIVE QUERIES

As we have seen, the semantics based on universal solutions is enough to compute the certain answers to any UCQ query. Therefore, the question regarding whether this semantics is also a good model for general queries arises. As shown in Arenas et al. [2004] and Libkin [2006], this semantics is not suitable for general queries, as it may give unintuitive answers even for simple data exchange settings.

Example 8.14   Consider the data exchange setting $M = (\{R\}, \{R'\}, \Sigma_{st}, \{\})$, where Σ_{st} simply copies the source instance into the target: $R(x, y) \rightarrow R'(x, y)$. Consider the source instance $I = \{R(a, b)\}$ and the query over the target schema $q(x, y) \leftarrow R'(x, y), \neg R'(x, x)$. Since one among all solutions is the instance $J = \{R(a, b), R(a, a)\}$, it follows that the set of certain answers is empty. However, this is not the expected behavior as the target instance should be just a copy of the source, and the "correct" certain answer should contain the set of tuples $\{R'(a, b)\}$. $\square$

In order to cope with problems related to general queries, the *closed world semantics* has been proposed for the data exchange problem. Libkin [2006] studies the problem for schema mappings containing only source to target TGDs and the set of universal solutions is replaced with the set of *CWA-solutions*. Intuitively, a *CWA*-solution satisfies certain requirements, which assert that every fact in the target instance is directly justified by the source instance and the source to target TGDs. *CWA-solutions* are in fact universal solutions, but the space of all solutions has two extreme points: the canonical universal solution and the core. A very good overview of the field, considering both relational and XML data, was recently provided by Arenas et al. [2010].

Hernich and Schweikardt [2007] extended the concept of *CWA*-solution to the case of schema mapping with target constraints and introduced a new chase based algorithm, called the α-*chase*, to compute *CWA-presolutions*, that are instances useful to compute the set of *CWA*-solutions. Moreover, Hernich [2011] adapted various classical semantics (Chan [1993], Minker [1982], Reiter [1978], Yahya and Henschen [1985]) for answering non-monotonic queries over incomplete data are adapted to the case of answering queries against the target schema. Each semantics is shown to be suitable for a certain class of queries and schema mappings. In fact, for each of these semantics, there are examples showing that the semantics leads to counter-intuitive answers or it does not respect logical equivalence of schema mappings. In addition, a new semantics, called *GCWA*-answers semantics*, is proposed, which seems to be well suited with respect to a number of schema mappings, including schema mappings defined by source to target TGDs and EGDs. We refer to [Hernich, 2010] for a complete overview of the problem of answering non-monotonic queries in data exchange.

BIBLIOGRAPHIC NOTES

The problem of conjunctive query containment was recognized fairly early as a fundamental problem in database query evaluation and optimization. In fact, conjunctive query containment can be used as a tool in query optimization, since query equivalence is reducible to query containment. Many papers point out that this problem is important in several contexts, including information integration [Ullman, 2000], query optimization [Abiteboul et al., 1995], materialized view maintenance [Gupta and Mumick, 1995], data warehousing [Widom, 1995], and constraint checking [Gupta et al., 1994].

Chandra and Merlin [1977] studied the computational complexity of conjunctive query containment and showed that it is an NP-complete problem. Complexity of other cases has also been studied, including intractability due to certain types of cycles in the query [Chekuri and Rajaraman, 1997], queries with inequalities [Klug, 1988], and various classes of Datalog queries with inequalities [Chaudhuri and Vardi, 1992].

Query containment under constraints has also been the subject of several investigations. Decidability of conjunctive query containment under functional and multi-valued dependencies was investigated by Aho et al. [1979b]; Johnson and Klug [1984] studied the problem under inclusion and functional dependencies, Dong and Su [1996] studied it for the case of constraints represented as a Datalog program, and Cali et al. [2008] studied it for guarder and weakly guarded TGDs.

The query containment problem is also the basis of the chase and backchase algorithm for query optimization. The method was originally proposed for enumerating the reformulations of a query under constraints [Deutsch et al., 1999]. However, query reformulation is also essential for data publishing [Deutsch and Tannen, 2003, Shanmugasundaram et al., 2001], and reformulation of XML queries, via a compilation from XML to relational queries and constraints [Deutsch and Tannen, 2003], as well as for schema evolution [Moon et al., 2008]. In addition, since views can be modeled as a pair of inclusion constraints, the chase and backchase algorithm also provides a technique for query rewriting with views [Levy et al., 1995], and hence is also applicable to information integration.

Data exchange was first introduced by Fagin et al. in their seminal paper [Fagin et al., 2005a], where they studied the semantics and the query answering problem. Fagin et al. [2005b] initiated the study of the computation of the core solution, and Gottlob and Nash [2008] proved that the problem of computing the core in the case of weakly acyclic target constraints can be done in PTIME. Successively, improved algorithms for the core computation were proposed by Mecca et al. [2009], ten Cate et al. [2009], Marnette [2009], Pichler and Savenkov [2010]. Moreover, as we have seen in Section 8.4, the problem of query answering in data exchange has been investigated a lot, especially the case of non-monotonic queries. The case of answering aggregate queries is addressed by Afrati and Kolaitis [2008]. The data exchange framework was also extended to peer-to-peer networks [Fuxman et al., 2005], to the case of incomplete data source [Afrati et al., 2008], source instances that may contain nulls [Fagin et al., 2011b], and in the presence of probabilistic data [Fagin et al., 2011a].

Data integration and data exchange are very similar, but the main difference is that, in data exchange, the data are indeed materialized at the target schema, which is not always the case for data integration settings. We refer the reader to [Lenzerini, 2002] and [Halevy et al., 2006] for a complete overview of the subject.

Several works have been done in the context of query answering in the presence of global constraints. In particular, we recall the work by Cali et al. [2004] on data integration in the presence of keys and foreign keys, where an algorithm for computing the certain answers to unions of conjunctive queries is provided. A more general result was given by Cali et al. [2003], where a practical algorithm based on query rewriting is proposed for answering unions of conjunctive queries in the presence of key dependencies and non-key-conflicting inclusion dependencies. Query answering in such a setting can be solved in PTIME in data complexity, whereas allowing inclusion dependencies that are not non-key-conflicting leads to undecidability of query answering [Cali et al., 2003].

Bibliography

Serge Abiteboul and Gosta Grahne. Update semantics for incomplete databases. In *Proc. 11th Int. Conf. on Very Large Data Bases*, pages 1–12, 1985. Cited on page(s) 18, 22

Serge Abiteboul, Paris C. Kanellakis, and Gosta Grahne. On the representation and querying of sets of possible worlds. *Theor. Comp. Sci.*, 78(1):158–187, 1991. DOI: 10.1016/0304-3975(51)90007-2 Cited on page(s) 22

Serge Abiteboul, Richard Hull, and Victor Vianu. *Foundations of Databases*. Addison-Wesley, 1995. Cited on page(s) 13, 22, 59, 95

Foto Afrati, Chen Li, and Vassia Pavlaki. Data exchange: query answering for incomplete data sources. In *Proc. 3rd Int. Conf. on Scalable Information Systems*, pages 6:1–6:10, 2008. DOI: 10.4108/ICST.INFOSCALE2008.3476 Cited on page(s) 95

Foto N. Afrati and Phokion G. Kolaitis. Answering aggregate queries in data exchange. In *Proc. 27th ACM SIGACT-SIGMOD-SIGART Symp. on Principles of Database Systems*, pages 129–138, 2008. DOI: 10.1145/1376916.1376936 Cited on page(s) 95

Foto N. Afrati and Phokion G. Kolaitis. Repair checking in inconsistent databases: algorithms and complexity. In *Proc. 12th Int. Conf. on Database Theory*, pages 31–41, 2009. DOI: 10.1145/1514894.1514899 Cited on page(s) 75, 77, 83, 85

Alfred V. Aho, Catriel Beeri, and Jeffrey D. Ullman. The theory of joins in relational databases. *ACM Trans. Database Syst.*, 4(3):297–314, 1979a. DOI: 10.1145/320083.320091 Cited on page(s) 25, 35, 64, 73

Alfred V. Aho, Yehoshua Sagiv, and Jeffrey D. Ullman. Equivalences among relational expressions. *SIAM J. on Comput.*, 8(2):218–246, 1979b. Cited on page(s) 35, 95

Periklis Andritsos, Ariel Fuxman, and Renée J. Miller. Clean answers over dirty databases: A probabilistic approach. In *Proc. 22nd Int. Conf. on Data Engineering*, page 30, 2006. DOI: 10.1109/ICDE.2006.35 Cited on page(s) 83

Lyublena Antova, Christoph Koch, and Dan Olteanu. $10^{(10^6)}$ worlds and beyond: efficient representation and processing of incomplete information. *VLDB J.*, 18(5):1021–1040, 2009. DOI: 10.1007/s00778-009-0149-y Cited on page(s) 22

98   BIBLIOGRAPHY

Marcelo Arenas, Leopoldo E. Bertossi, and Jan Chomicki. Consistent query answers in inconsistent databases. In *Proc. 18th ACM SIGACT-SIGMOD-SIGART Symp. on Principles of Database Systems*, pages 68–79, 1999. DOI: 10.1145/303976.303983 Cited on page(s) 75, 77, 82, 83, 85

Marcelo Arenas, Pablo Barceló, Ronald Fagin, and Leonid Libkin. Locally consistent transformations and query answering in data exchange. In *Proc. 23rd ACM SIGACT-SIGMOD-SIGART Symp. on Principles of Database Systems*, pages 229–240, 2004. DOI: 10.1145/1055558.1055592 Cited on page(s) 94

Marcelo Arenas, Pablo Barceló, Leonid Libkin, and Filip Murlak. *Relational and XML Data Exchange*. Morgan & Claypool Publishers, 2010.
DOI: 10.2200/S00297ED1V01Y201008DTM008 Cited on page(s) 94

William Ward Armstrong. Dependency structures of data base relationships. In *Proceedings of IFIP Congress, Information Processing 74*, pages 580–583, 1974. Cited on page(s) 1, 60

Paolo Atzeni and Nicola M. Morfuni. Functional dependencies and constraints on null values in database relations. *Information and Control*, 70(1):1–31, 1986.
DOI: 10.1016/S0019-9958(86)80022-5 Cited on page(s) 22

Pablo Barceló, Leonid Libkin, and Miguel Romero. Efficient approximations of conjunctive queries. In *PODS*, pages 249–260, 2012. DOI: 10.1145/2213556.2213591 Cited on page(s) 13

Catriel Beeri and Moshe Y. Vardi. A proof procedure for data dependencies. *J. ACM*, 31(4):718–741, 1984. DOI: 10.1145/1634.1636 Cited on page(s) 35, 58, 71, 73

Catriel Beeri, Ronald Fagin, and John H. Howard. A complete axiomatization for functional and multivalued dependencies in database relations. In *Proc. ACM SIGMOD Int. Conf. on Management of Data*, pages 47–61, 1977. DOI: 10.1145/509404.509414 Cited on page(s) 72

Catriel Beeri, Alberto O. Mendelzon, Yehoshua Sagiv, and Jeffrey D. Ullman. Equivalence of relational database schemes. *SIAM J. on Comput.*, 10(2):352–370, 1981. DOI: 10.1137/0210025 Cited on page(s) 73

Philip A. Bernstein. Synthesizing third normal form relations from functional dependencies. *ACM Trans. Database Syst.*, 1(4):277–298, 1976. DOI: 10.1145/320493.320489 Cited on page(s) 1

Leopoldo E. Bertossi. Consistent query answering in databases. *ACM SIGMOD Rec.*, 35(2):68–76, 2006. DOI: 10.1145/1147376.1147391 Cited on page(s) 75, 83

Leopoldo E. Bertossi. *Database Repairing and Consistent Query Answering*. Morgan & Claypool Publishers, 2011. DOI: 10.2200/S00379ED1V01Y201108DTM020 Cited on page(s) 75, 83

Leopoldo E. Bertossi and Loreto Bravo. Consistent query answers in virtual data integration systems. In *Inconsistency Tolerance*, pages 42–83, 2005. DOI: 10.1007/b104925 Cited on page(s) 91

Leopoldo E. Bertossi and Loreto Bravo. The semantics of consistency and trust in peer data exchange systems. In *Proc. 14th Int. Conf. Logic for Programming, Artificial Intelligence, and Reasoning*, pages 107–122, 2007. DOI: 10.1007/978-3-540-75560-9_10 Cited on page(s) 23

Leopoldo E. Bertossi and Lechen Li. Achieving data privacy through secrecy views and null-based virtual updates. *CoRR*, 2011. Cited on page(s) 23

Leopoldo E. Bertossi, Loreto Bravo, Enrico Franconi, and Andrei Lopatenko. The complexity and approximation of fixing numerical attributes in databases under integrity constraints. *Inf. Syst.*, 33(4-5):407–434, 2008. DOI: 10.1016/j.is.2008.01.005 Cited on page(s) 75, 82

Joachim Biskup. A formal approach to null values in database relations. In *Advances in Data Base Theory*, pages 299–341, 1979. Cited on page(s) 22

Philip Bohannon, Michael Flaster, Wenfei Fan, and Rajeev Rastogi. A cost-based model and effective heuristic for repairing constraints by value modification. In *Proc. ACM SIGMOD Int. Conf. on Management of Data*, pages 143–154, 2005. DOI: 10.1145/1066157.1066175 Cited on page(s) 82

Loreto Bravo and Leopoldo E. Bertossi. Logic programs for consistently querying data integration systems. In *Proc. 18th Int. Joint Conf. on AI*, pages 10–15, 2003. Cited on page(s) 91

Loreto Bravo and Leopoldo E. Bertossi. Semantically correct query answers in the presence of null values. In *EDBT Workshops*, pages 336–357, 2006. DOI: 10.1007/11896548_27 Cited on page(s) 23

Andrea Cali and Andreas Pieris. On equality-generating dependencies in ontology querying - preliminary report. In *Proc. 5th Alberto Mendelzon Int. Workshop on Foundations of Data Management*, 2011. Cited on page(s) 94

Andrea Cali, Domenico Lembo, and Riccardo Rosati. On the decidability and complexity of query answering over inconsistent and incomplete databases. In *Proc. 22nd ACM SIGACT-SIGMOD-SIGART Symp. on Principles of Database Systems*, pages 260–271, 2003. DOI: 10.1145/773153.773179 Cited on page(s) 77, 93, 94, 96

Andrea Cali, Diego Calvanese, Giuseppe De Giacomo, and Maurizio Lenzerini. Data integration under integrity constraints. *Inf. Syst.*, 29(2):147–163, 2004. DOI: 10.1016/S0306-4379(03)00050-4 Cited on page(s) 85, 91, 96

Andrea Cali, Georg Gottlob, and Michael Kifer. Taming the infinite chase: Query answering under expressive relational constraints. In *Proc. 21st Int. Workshop on Description Logics*, 2008. Cited on page(s) 29, 31, 33, 42, 92, 93, 95

Andrea Cali, Georg Gottlob, and Thomas Lukasiewicz. A general datalog-based framework for tractable query answering over ontologies. In *Proc. 28th ACM SIGACT-SIGMOD-SIGART Symp. on Principles of Database Systems*, pages 77–86, 2009a. DOI: 10.1145/1559795.1559809 Cited on page(s) 1, 85, 93, 94

Andrea Cali, Georg Gottlob, and Thomas Lukasiewicz. Datalog$^{\pm}$: a unified approach to ontologies and integrity constraints. In *Proc. 12th Int. Conf. on Database Theory*, pages 14–30, 2009b. DOI: 10.1145/1514894.1514897 Cited on page(s) 1, 85

Andrea Cali, Georg Gottlob, and Andreas Pieris. Advanced processing for ontological queries. *Proc. VLDB Endowment*, 3(1):554–565, 2010. Cited on page(s) 93, 94

Luciano Caroprese, Sergio Greco, and Ester Zumpano. Active integrity constraints for database consistency maintenance. *IEEE Trans. Knowl. and Data Eng.*, 21(7):1042–1058, 2009. DOI: 10.1109/TKDE.2008.226 Cited on page(s) 75

Marco A. Casanova, Ronald Fagin, and Christos H. Papadimitriou. Inclusion dependencies and their interaction with functional dependencies. *J. Comp. and System Sci.*, 28(1):29–59, 1984. DOI: 10.1016/0022-0000(84)90075-8 Cited on page(s) 58, 71, 87

Edward P. F. Chan. A possible world semantics for disjunctive databases. *IEEE Trans. Knowl. and Data Eng.*, 5(2):282–292, 1993. DOI: 10.1109/69.219736 Cited on page(s) 94

Ashok K. Chandra and Philip M. Merlin. Optimal implementation of conjunctive queries in relational data bases. In *Proc. 9th Annual ACM Symp. on Theory of Computing*, pages 77–90, 1977. DOI: 10.1145/800105.803397 Cited on page(s) 13, 95

Surajit Chaudhuri and Moshe Y. Vardi. On the equivalence of recursive and nonrecursive datalog programs. In *Proc. 11th ACM SIGACT-SIGMOD-SIGART Symp. on Principles of Database Systems*, pages 55–66, 1992. DOI: 10.1145/137097.137109 Cited on page(s) 95

Chandra Chekuri and Anand Rajaraman. Conjunctive query containment revisited. In *Proc. 6th Int. Conf. on Database Theory*, pages 56–70, 1997. DOI: 10.1007/3-540-62222-5_36 Cited on page(s) 95

Jan Chomicki. Consistent query answering: Five easy pieces. In *Proc. 11th Int. Conf. on Database Theory*, pages 1–17, 2007. DOI: 10.1007/11965893_1 Cited on page(s) 75, 77, 83

Jan Chomicki and Jerzy Marcinkowski. Minimal-change integrity maintenance using tuple deletions. *Information and Comput.*, 197(1-2):90–121, 2005. DOI: 10.1016/j.ic.2004.04.007 Cited on page(s) 75, 77

E. F. Codd. Further normalizations of the database relational model. In *Courant Computer Science Synopsia 6: Data Base Systems*, pages 33–64. Prentice Hall, 1972. Cited on page(s) 1, 13, 72

E. F. Codd. Recent investigations in relational data base systems. In *Proceedings of IFIP Congress, Information Processing 74*, pages 1017–1021, 1974. Cited on page(s) 72

E. F. Codd. Extending the database relational model to capture more meaning. *ACM Trans. Database Syst.*, 4(4):397–434, 1979. DOI: 10.1145/320107.320109 Cited on page(s) 22

Edgar F. Codd. A relational model of data for large shared data banks. *Commun. ACM*, 13(6): 377–387, 1970. DOI: 10.1145/362384.362685 Cited on page(s) 3, 13

Sara Cohen, Werner Nutt, and Yehoshua Sagiv. Deciding equivalences among conjunctive aggregate queries. *J. ACM*, 54(2), 2007. DOI: 10.1145/1219092.1219093 Cited on page(s) 13

Nilesh N. Dalvi and Dan Suciu. The dichotomy of conjunctive queries on probabilistic structures. In *PODS*, pages 293–302, 2007. DOI: 10.1145/1265530.1265571 Cited on page(s) 13

Hugh Darwen, C. J. Date, and Ronald Fagin. A normal form for preventing redundant tuples in relational databases. In *Proc. 15th Int. Conf. on Database Theory*, pages 129–142, 2012. DOI: 10.1145/2274576.2274589 Cited on page(s) 1, 66, 68, 69, 70, 73

Chris J. Date. *An introduction to database systems (7. ed.)*. Addison-Wesley-Longman, 2000. Cited on page(s) 13, 59

Alin Deutsch and Val Tannen. Reformulation of xml queries and constraints. In *Proc. 9th Int. Conf. on Database Theory*, pages 225–241, 2003. DOI: 10.1007/3-540-36285-1_15 Cited on page(s) 38, 58, 95

Alin Deutsch, Lucian Popa, and Val Tannen. Physical data independence, constraints, and optimization with universal plans. In *Proc. 25th Int. Conf. on Very Large Data Bases*, pages 459–470, 1999. Cited on page(s) 36, 88, 95

Alin Deutsch, Lucian Popa, and Val Tannen. Query reformulation with constraints. *ACM SIGMOD Rec.*, 35(1):65–73, 2006. DOI: 10.1145/1121995.1122010 Cited on page(s) 36, 88

Alin Deutsch, Alan Nash, and Jeffrey B. Remmel. The chase revisited. In *Proc. 27th ACM SIGACT-SIGMOD-SIGART Symp. on Principles of Database Systems*, pages 149–158, 2008. DOI: 10.1145/1376916.1376938 Cited on page(s) 29, 31, 33, 34, 35, 36, 39, 40, 50, 58, 86, 92

Guozhu Dong and Jianwen Su. Conjunctive query containment with respect to views and constraints. *Inf. Proc. Letters*, 57(2):95–102, 1996. DOI: 10.1016/0020-0190(95)00192-1 Cited on page(s) 95

Oliver M. Duschka and Alon Y. Levy. Recursive plans for information gathering. In *Proc. 15th Int. Joint Conf. on AI*, pages 778–784, 1997. Cited on page(s) 90

Ramez Elmasri and Shamkant B. Navathe. *Fundamentals of Database Systems, 3rd Edition*. Addison-Wesley-Longman, 2000. Cited on page(s) 13, 59

Ronald Fagin. The decomposition versus synthetic approach to relational database design. In *Proc. 3rd Int. Conf. on Very Data Bases*, pages 441–446, 1977a. Cited on page(s) 73

Ronald Fagin. Multivalued dependencies and a new normal form for relational databases. *ACM Trans. Database Syst.*, 2(3):262–278, 1977b. DOI: 10.1145/320557.320571 Cited on page(s) 1, 72

Ronald Fagin. Normal forms and relational database operators. In *Proc. ACM SIGMOD Int. Conf. on Management of Data*, pages 153–160, 1979. DOI: 10.1145/582095.582120 Cited on page(s) 63, 66, 68, 73

Ronald Fagi and Moshe Vardi (1986) The Theory of Data Dependencies - a Survey, *Proc. of Symposia in Applied Mathematics*, 34 19–71, 1986. Cited on page(s) 1

Ronald Fagin, Phokion G. Kolaitis, Renée J. Miller, and Lucian Popa. Data exchange: Semantics and query answering. In *Proc. 9th Int. Conf. on Database Theory*, pages 207–224, 2003. DOI: 10.1007/3-540-36285-1_14 Cited on page(s) 58

Ronald Fagin, Phokion G. Kolaitis, Renée J. Miller, and Lucian Popa. Data exchange: semantics and query answering. *Theor. Comp. Sci.*, 336(1):89–124, 2005a. DOI: 10.1016/j.tcs.2004.10.033 Cited on page(s) 1, 26, 27, 29, 30, 38, 39, 85, 88, 91, 95

Ronald Fagin, Phokion G. Kolaitis, and Lucian Popa. Data exchange: getting to the core. *ACM Trans. Database Syst.*, 30(1):174–210, 2005b. DOI: 10.1145/1061318.1061323 Cited on page(s) 27, 95

Ronald Fagin, Benny Kimelfeld, and Phokion G. Kolaitis. Probabilistic data exchange. *J. ACM*, 58 (4):15, 2011a. DOI: 10.1145/1989727.1989729 Cited on page(s) 95

Ronald Fagin, Phokion G. Kolaitis, Lucian Popa, and Wang Chiew Tan. Reverse data exchange: Coping with nulls. *ACM Trans. Database Syst.*, 36(2):11, 2011b. DOI: 10.1145/1966385.1966389 Cited on page(s) 95

Sergio Flesca, Filippo Furfaro, Sergio Greco, and Ester Zumpano. Repairs and consistent answers for xml data with functional dependencies. In *Proc. 1st Int. XML Database Symp. on Database and XML Technologies*, pages 238–253, 2003. DOI: 10.1007/978-3-540-39429-7_16 Cited on page(s) 83

Sergio Flesca, Filippo Furfaro, and Francesco Parisi. Querying and repairing inconsistent numerical databases. *ACM Trans. Database Syst.*, 35(2), 2010. DOI: 10.1145/1735886.1735893 Cited on page(s) 75, 82

Enrico Franconi and Sergio Tessaris. On the logic of sql nulls. In *Proc. 6th Alberto Mendelzon Int. Workshop on Foundations of Data Management*, pages 114–128, 2012a. Cited on page(s) 23

Enrico Franconi and Sergio Tessaris. The algebra and the logic for sql nulls. In *Proc. 20th Italian Symposium on Advanced Database Systems*, pages 163–175, 2012b. Cited on page(s) 23

Filippo Furfaro, Sergio Greco, and Cristian Molinaro. A three-valued semantics for querying and repairing inconsistent databases. *Ann. Math. Artif. Intell.*, 51(2-4):167–193, 2007. DOI: 10.1007/s10472-008-9088-3 Cited on page(s) 82

Ariel Fuxman and Renée J. Miller. First-order query rewriting for inconsistent databases. *J. Comp. and System Sci.*, 73(4):610–635, 2007. DOI: 10.1016/j.jcss.2006.10.013 Cited on page(s) 75, 78, 83

Ariel Fuxman, Phokion G. Kolaitis, Renée J. Miller, and Wang Chiew Tan. Peer data exchange. In *Proc. 24th ACM SIGACT-SIGMOD-SIGART Symp. on Principles of Database Systems*, pages 160–171, 2005. DOI: 10.1145/1065167.1065188 Cited on page(s) 85, 95

Hector Garcia-Molina, Jeffrey D. Ullman, and Jennifer Widom. *Database systems - the complete book (2. ed.)*. Pearson Education, 2009. Cited on page(s) 13, 59

Georg Gottlob and Alan Nash. Efficient core computation in data exchange. *J. ACM*, 55(2), 2008. DOI: 10.1145/1346330.1346334 Cited on page(s) 27, 32, 95

Georg Gottlob, Nicola Leone, and Francesco Scarcello. The complexity of acyclic conjunctive queries. *J. ACM*, 48(3):431–498, 2001. DOI: 10.1145/382780.382783 Cited on page(s) 13

Georg Gottlob, Christoph Koch, and Klaus U. Schulz. Conjunctive queries over trees. *J. ACM*, 53 (2):238–272, 2006. DOI: 10.1145/1131342.1131345 Cited on page(s) 13

Gosta Grahne. Dependency satisfaction in databases with incomplete information. In *Proc. 10th Int. Conf. on Very Large Data Bases*, pages 37–45, 1984. Cited on page(s) 18

Gosta Grahne. *The Problem of Incomplete Information in Relational Databases*. Springer, 1991. DOI: 10.1007/3-540-54919-6 Cited on page(s) 22

Gosta Grahne and Adrian Onet. Data correspondence, exchange and repair. In *Proc. 13th Int. Conf. on Database Theory*, pages 219–230, 2010. DOI: 10.1145/1804669.1804698 Cited on page(s) 75, 85

Gosta Grahne and Adrian Onet. On conditional chase termination. In *Proc. 5th Alberto Mendelzon Int. Workshop on Foundations of Data Management*, 2011. Cited on page(s) 38, 39

John Grant. Null values in a relational data base. *Inf. Proc. Letters*, 6(5):156–157, 1977. DOI: 10.1016/0020-0190(77)90013-8 Cited on page(s) 22

Gianluigi Greco, Sergio Greco, and Ester Zumpano. A logical framework for querying and repairing inconsistent databases. *IEEE Trans. Knowl. and Data Eng.*, 15(6):1389–1408, 2003. DOI: 10.1109/TKDE.2003.1245280 Cited on page(s) 75, 77

Sergio Greco and Cristian Molinaro. Probabilistic query answering over inconsistent databases. *Ann. Math. Artif. Intell.*, 64(2-3):185–207, 2012. DOI: 10.1007/s10472-012-9287-9 Cited on page(s) 75, 83

Sergio Greco and Francesca Spezzano. Chase termination: A constraints rewriting approach. *Proc. VLDB Endowment*, 3(1):93–104, 2010. Cited on page(s) 46, 50, 51, 53, 56, 58

Sergio Greco, Francesca Spezzano, and Irina Trubitsyna. Stratification criteria and rewriting techniques for checking chase termination. *Proc. VLDB Endowment*, 4(11):1158–1168, 2011. Cited on page(s) 1, 47, 48, 49, 50, 51, 52, 53, 56, 57, 58

Ashish Gupta and Inderpal Singh Mumick. Maintenance of materialized views: Problems, techniques, and applications. *Q. Bull. IEEE TC on Data Eng.*, 18(2):3–18, 1995. Cited on page(s) 95

Ashish Gupta, Yehoshua Sagiv, Jeffrey D. Ullman, and Jennifer Widom. Constraint checking with partial information. In *Proc. 13th ACM SIGACT-SIGMOD-SIGART Symp. on Principles of Database Systems*, pages 45–55, 1994. DOI: 10.1145/182591.182597 Cited on page(s) 95

Alon Y. Halevy, Anand Rajaraman, and Joann J. Ordille. Data integration: The teenage years. In *Proc. 32nd Int. Conf. on Very Large Data Bases*, pages 9–16, 2006. Cited on page(s) 96

Sven Hartmann and Sebastian Link. When data dependencies over sql tables meet the logics of paradox and s-3. In *Proc. 29th ACM SIGACT-SIGMOD-SIGART Symp. on Principles of Database Systems*, pages 317–326, 2010. DOI: 10.1145/1807085.1807126 Cited on page(s) 22

Sven Hartmann and Sebastian Link. The implication problem of data dependencies over sql table definitions: Axiomatic, algorithmic and logical characterizations. *ACM Trans. Database Syst.*, 37 (2), 2012. DOI: 10.1145/2188349.2188355 Cited on page(s) 22

Sven Hartmann, Markus Kirchberg, and Sebastian Link. Design by example for sql table definitions with functional dependencies. *VLDB J.*, 21(1):121–144, 2012. DOI: 10.1007/s00778-011-0239-5 Cited on page(s) 22

André Hernich. *Foundations of query answering in relational data exchange*. PhD thesis, 2010. Cited on page(s) 94

André Hernich. Answering non-monotonic queries in relational data exchange. *Logical Methods in Computer Science*, 7(3), 2011. DOI: 10.1145/1804669.1804688 Cited on page(s) 94

André Hernich and Nicole Schweikardt. Cwa-solutions for data exchange settings with target dependencies. In *Proc. 26th ACM SIGACT-SIGMOD-SIGART Symp. on Principles of Database Systems*, pages 113–122, 2007. DOI: 10.1145/1265530.1265547 Cited on page(s) 36, 39, 94

Richard Hull and Masatoshi Yoshikawa. Ilog: Declarative creation and manipulation of object identifiers. In *Proc. 16th Int. Conf. on Very Large Data Bases*, pages 455–468, 1990. Cited on page(s) 38

Tomasz Imielinski and Witold Lipski. On representing incomplete information in a relational data base. In *Proc. 7th Int. Conf. on Very Data Bases*, pages 388–397, 1981. Cited on page(s) 22

Tomasz Imielinski and Witold Lipski. Incomplete information and dependencies in relational databases. In *Proc. ACM SIGMOD Int. Conf. on Management of Data*, pages 178–184, 1983. DOI: 10.1145/971695.582222 Cited on page(s) 22

Tomasz Imielinski and Witold Lipski. Incomplete information in relational databases. *J. ACM*, 31 (4):761–791, 1984. DOI: 10.1145/1634.1886 Cited on page(s) 18, 22

Tomasz Imielinski, Ron van der Meyden, and Kumar V. Vadaparty. Complexity tailored design: A new design methodology for databases with incomplete information. *J. Comp. and System Sci.*, 51 (3):405–432, 1995. DOI: 10.1006/jcss.1995.1079 Cited on page(s) 22

David S. Johnson and Anthony C. Klug. Testing containment of conjunctive queries under functional and inclusion dependencies. *J. Comp. and System Sci.*, 28(1):167–189, 1984. DOI: 10.1016/0022-0000(84)90081-3 Cited on page(s) 13, 86, 87, 95

Gregory Karvounarakis and Val Tannen. Conjunctive queries and mappings with unequalities. Technical report, CIS - University of Pennsylvania, 2008. Cited on page(s) 36

Anthony C. Klug. On conjunctive queries containing inequalities. *J. ACM*, 35(1):146–160, 1988. DOI: 10.1145/42267.42273 Cited on page(s) 13, 95

Phokion G. Kolaitis and Moshe Y. Vardi. Conjunctive-query containment and constraint satisfaction. *J. Comp. and System Sci.*, 61(2):302–332, 2000. DOI: 10.1006/jcss.2000.1713 Cited on page(s) 1, 13

Paraschos Koutris and Dan Suciu. Parallel evaluation of conjunctive queries. In *PODS*, pages 223–234, 2011. DOI: 10.1145/1989284.1989310 Cited on page(s) 13

Maurizio Lenzerini. Data integration: A theoretical perspective. In *Proc. 21st ACM SIGACT-SIGMOD-SIGART Symp. on Principles of Database Systems*, pages 233–246, 2002. DOI: 10.1145/543613.543644 Cited on page(s) 1, 85, 90, 96

Mark Levene and George Loizou. Axiomatisation of functional dependencies in incomplete relations. *Theor. Comp. Sci.*, 206(1-2):283–300, 1998. DOI: 10.1016/S0304-3975(98)80029-7 Cited on page(s) 22

Mark Levene and George Loizou. Database design for incomplete relations. *ACM Trans. Database Syst.*, 24(1):80–125, 1999. DOI: 10.1145/310701.310712 Cited on page(s) 22

Alon Y. Levy, Alberto O. Mendelzon, Yehoshua Sagiv, and Divesh Srivastava. Answering queries using views. In *Proc. 14th ACM SIGACT-SIGMOD-SIGART Symp. on Principles of Database Systems*, pages 95–104, 1995. DOI: 10.1145/1013202.1013204 Cited on page(s) 95

Leonid Libkin. Data exchange and incomplete information. In *Proc. 25th ACM SIGACT-SIGMOD-SIGART Symp. on Principles of Database Systems*, pages 60–69, 2006. DOI: 10.1145/1142351.1142360 Cited on page(s) 36, 94

Y. Edmund Lien. On the equivalence of database models. *J. ACM*, 29(2):333–362, 1982. DOI: 10.1145/322307.322311 Cited on page(s) 22

Witold Lipski. On semantic issues connected with incomplete information databases. *ACM Trans. Database Syst.*, 4(3):262–296, 1979. DOI: 10.1145/320083.320088 Cited on page(s) 22

Witold Lipski. On relational algebra with marked nulls. In *Proc. 3rd ACM SIGACT-SIGMOD Symp. on Principles of Database Systems*, pages 201–203, 1984. DOI: 10.1145/588011.588040 Cited on page(s) 22

John W. Lloyd. *Foundations of Logic Programming, 1st Edition*. Springer, 1984. DOI: 10.1007/978-3-642-96826-6 Cited on page(s) 13

Andrei Lopatenko and Leopoldo E. Bertossi. Complexity of consistent query answering in databases under cardinality-based and incremental repair semantics. In *Proc. 11th Int. Conf. on Database Theory*, pages 179–193, 2007. DOI: 10.1007/11965893_13 Cited on page(s) 75, 82

David Maier. *The Theory of Relational Databases*. Computer Science Press, 1983. Cited on page(s) 13, 59, 67, 68, 73

David Maier, Alberto O. Mendelzon, and Yehoshua Sagiv. Testing implications of data dependencies. *ACM Trans. Database Syst.*, 4(4):455–469, 1979. DOI: 10.1145/320107.320115 Cited on page(s) 1, 25, 35, 71, 73

David Maier, Yehoshua Sagiv, and Mihalis Yannakakis. On the complexity of testing implications of functional and join dependencies. *J. ACM*, 28(4):680–695, 1981. DOI: 10.1145/322276.322280 Cited on page(s) 35

Bruno Marnette. Generalized schema-mappings: from termination to tractability. In *Proc. 28th ACM SIGACT-SIGMOD-SIGART Symp. on Principles of Database Systems*, pages 13–22, 2009. DOI: 10.1145/1559795.1559799 Cited on page(s) 29, 31, 32, 34, 35, 45, 46, 58, 95

Bruno Marnette and Floris Geerts. Static analysis of schema-mappings ensuring oblivious termination. In *Proc. 13th Int. Conf. on Database Theory*, pages 183–195, 2010. DOI: 10.1145/1804669.1804694 Cited on page(s) 36, 58

Giansalvatore Mecca, Paolo Papotti, and Salvatore Raunich. Core schema mappings. In *Proc. ACM SIGMOD Int. Conf. on Management of Data*, pages 655–668, 2009. DOI: 10.1145/1559845.1559914 Cited on page(s) 27, 95

Michael Meier. *On the Termination of the Chase Algorithm.* Albert-Ludwigs-Universität Freiburg (Germany), 2010. Cited on page(s) 44, 51, 58

Michael Meier, Michael Schmidt, and Georg Lausen. On chase termination beyond stratification. *Proc. VLDB Endowment*, 2(1):970–981, 2009a. Cited on page(s) 29, 31, 32, 42, 43, 44, 45, 58

Michael Meier, Michael Schmidt, and Georg Lausen. On chase termination beyond stratification. *CoRR*, abs/0906.4228, 2009b. Cited on page(s) 41, 43, 44, 45, 50, 58

Jack Minker. On indefinite databases and the closed world assumption. In *Proc. 6th Conf. on Automated Deduction*, pages 292–308, 1982. DOI: 10.1007/BFb0000066 Cited on page(s) 94

Jack Minker, editor. *Foundations of Deductive Databases and Logic Programming*. Morgan Kaufmann, 1988. Cited on page(s) 13

Cristian Molinaro and Sergio Greco. Polynomial time queries over inconsistent databases with functional dependencies and foreign keys. *Data & Knowl. Eng.*, 69(7):709–722, 2010. DOI: 10.1016/j.datak.2010.02.007 Cited on page(s) 75

Hyun Jin Moon, Carlo Curino, Alin Deutsch, Chien-Yi Hou, and Carlo Zaniolo. Managing and querying transaction-time databases under schema evolution. *Proc. VLDB Endowment*, 1(1): 882–895, 2008. DOI: 10.1145/1453856.1453952 Cited on page(s) 95

Ragnar Normann. Minimal lossless decompositions and some normal forms between 4nf and pj/nf. *Inf. Syst.*, 23(7):509–516, 1998. DOI: 10.1016/S0306-4379(98)00025-8 Cited on page(s) 68, 73

Adrian Constantin Onet. *The chase procedure and its applications.* PhD thesis, Department of Computer Science and Software Engineering, Concordia University, Montreal, Quebec, Canada, 2012. Cited on page(s) 35

Sergey V. Petrov. Finite axiomatisation of languages for representation of system properties. *Inf. Sci.*, 47(3):339–372, 1989. DOI: 10.1016/0020-0255(89)90006-6 Cited on page(s) 63

Reinhard Pichler and Vadim Savenkov. Towards practical feasibility of core computation in data exchange. *Theor. Comp. Sci.*, 411(7-9):935–957, 2010. DOI: 10.1016/j.tcs.2009.09.035 Cited on page(s) 95

Lucian Popa, Alin Deutsch, Arnaud Sahuguet, and Val Tannen. A chase too far? In *Proc. ACM SIGMOD Int. Conf. on Management of Data*, pages 273–284, 2000. DOI: 10.1145/335191.335421 Cited on page(s) 36, 88

Raghu Ramakrishnan and Johannes Gehrke. *Database management systems (3. ed.)*. McGraw-Hill, 2003. Cited on page(s) 13, 59

Raymond Reiter. On closed world data bases. In *Logic and Data Bases*, pages 55–76. Plenum Press, 1978. DOI: 10.1007/978-1-4684-3384-5_3 Cited on page(s) 94

Raymond Reiter. A sound and sometimes complete query evaluation algorithm for relational databases with null values. *J. ACM*, 33(2):349–370, 1986. DOI: 10.1145/5383.5388 Cited on page(s) 22

Jorma Rissanen. Independent components of relations. *ACM Trans. Database Syst.*, 2(4):317–325, 1977. DOI: 10.1145/320576.320580 Cited on page(s) 73

M. Andrea Rodríguez, Leopoldo E. Bertossi, and Mónica Caniupán Marileo. An inconsistency tolerant approach to querying spatial databases. In *Proc. 16th SIGSPATIAL ACM Int. Symp. on Advances in Geographic Information Systems*, page 36, 2008. DOI: 10.1145/1463434.1463480 Cited on page(s) 83

M. Andrea Rodríguez, Leopoldo E. Bertossi, and Mónica Caniupán Marileo. Consistent query answering under spatial semantic constraints. *CoRR*, abs/1106.1478, 2011. Cited on page(s) 83

Anish Das Sarma, Omar Benjelloun, Alon Y. Halevy, Shubha U. Nabar, and Jennifer Widom. Representing uncertain data: models, properties, and algorithms. *VLDB J.*, 18(5):989–1019, 2009. DOI: 10.1007/s00778-009-0147-0 Cited on page(s) 23

Jayavel Shanmugasundaram, Jerry Kiernan, Eugene J. Shekita, Catalina Fan, and John E. Funder-burk. Querying xml views of relational data. In *Proc. 27th Int. Conf. on Very Large Data Bases*, pages 261–270, 2001. Cited on page(s) 95

Abraham Silberschatz, Henry F. Korth, and S. Sudarshan. *Database System Concepts, 6th Edition*. McGraw-Hill Book Company, 2010. Cited on page(s) 13, 59, 66

Slawomir Staworko and Jan Chomicki. Validity-sensitive querying of xml databases. In *EDBT Workshops*, pages 164–177, 2006. DOI: 10.1007/11896548_16 Cited on page(s) 83

Slawomir Staworko and Jan Chomicki. Consistent query answers in the presence of universal constraints. *Inf. Syst.*, 35(1):1–22, 2010. DOI: 10.1016/j.is.2009.03.004 Cited on page(s) 77

Balder ten Cate, Laura Chiticariu, Phokion G. Kolaitis, and Wang Chiew Tan. Laconic schema mappings: Computing the core with sql queries. *Proc. VLDB Endowment*, 2(1):1006–1017, 2009. Cited on page(s) 27, 29, 31, 95

Balder ten Cate, Gaelle Fontaine, and Phokion G. Kolaitis. On the data complexity of consistent query answering. In *Proc. 15th Int. Conf. on Database Theory*, 2012. DOI: 10.1145/2274576.2274580 Cited on page(s) 1, 78, 80, 81, 82, 83

Jeffrey D. Ullman. *Principles of Database and Knowledge-Base Systems, Volume I.* Computer Science Press, 1988. Cited on page(s) 13, 59

Jeffrey D. Ullman. Information integration using logical views. *Theor. Comp. Sci.*, 239(2):189–210, 2000. DOI: 10.1016/S0304-3975(99)00219-4 Cited on page(s) 95

Moshe Y. Vardi. Fundamentals of dependency theory. In *Trends in Theoretical Computer Science*, 1988. DOI: 10.1007/11537311_31 Cited on page(s) 1

Moshe Y. Vardi. Inferring multivalued dependencies from functional and join dependencies. *Acta Informatica*, 19:305–324, 1983. DOI: 10.1007/BF00290729 Cited on page(s) 35

Moshe Y. Vardi. The implication and finite implication problems for typed template dependencies. *J. Comp. and System Sci.*, 28(1):3–28, 1984. DOI: 10.1016/0022-0000(84)90074-6 Cited on page(s) 77

Yannis Vassiliou. Functional dependencies and incomplete information. In *Proc. 6th Int. Conf. on Very Data Bases*, pages 260–269, 1980. Cited on page(s) 22

Millist W. Vincent. A corrected 5nf definition for relational database design. *Theor. Comp. Sci.*, 185 (2):379–391, 1997. DOI: 10.1016/S0304-3975(97)00050-9 Cited on page(s) 67, 68, 73

Jennifer Widom. Letter from the special issue editor. *Q. Bull. IEEE TC on Data Eng.*, 18(2):2, 1995. Cited on page(s) 95

Jef Wijsen. Database repairing using updates. *ACM Trans. Database Syst.*, 30(3):722–768, 2005. DOI: 10.1145/1093382.1093385 Cited on page(s) 75, 82

Jef Wijsen. On the first-order expressibility of computing certain answers to conjunctive queries over uncertain databases. In *Proc. 29th ACM SIGACT-SIGMOD-SIGART Symp. on Principles of Database Systems*, pages 179–190, 2010. DOI: 10.1145/1807085.1807111 Cited on page(s) 13, 75, 77, 78, 83

Mahkameh Yaghmaie, Leopoldo Bertossi, and Sina Ariyan. Repair-oriented relational schemas for multidimensional databases. In *Proc. 15th Int. Conf. on Extending Database Technology*, 2012. DOI: 10.1145/2247596.2247644 Cited on page(s) 83

Adnan H. Yahya and Lawrence J. Henschen. Deduction in non-horn databases. *J. Autom. Reasoning*, 1(2):141–160, 1985. DOI: 10.1007/BF00244994 Cited on page(s) 94

Li-Yan Yuan and Ding-An Chiang. A sound and complete query evaluation algorithm for relational databases with null values. In *Proc. ACM SIGMOD Int. Conf. on Management of Data*, pages 74–81, 1988. DOI: 10.1145/971701.50210 Cited on page(s) 22

Carlo Zaniolo. *Analysis and Design of Relational Schemata for Database Systems.* Doctoral diss., UCLA, Los Angeles, CA, 1976. Cited on page(s) 72

Carlo Zaniolo. Database relations with null values. *J. Comp. and System Sci.*, 28(1):142–166, 1984. DOI: 10.1016/0022-0000(84)90080-1 Cited on page(s) 22

Authors' Biographies

SERGIO GRECO

Sergio Greco is a full professor and chair of the Department of Electronics, Computer and System Science at the University of Calabria (Italy). He was an assistant professor (1988-1998) and associate professor (1998-2000) at the University of Calabria, as well as a visiting researcher at the Microelectronics and Computer Corporation of Austin (1990-1991) and at the of University of California at Los Angeles (1996, and again in 1998). Currently he is an Associate Editor of the *IEEE Transaction of Knowledge and Data Engineering Journal.* Professor Greco's research interests include database theory, data integration, inconsistent data, data mining, knowledge representation, logic programming, and computational logic.

CRISTIAN MOLINARO

Cristian Molinaro received a Ph.D. degree in Computer Science Engineering from the University of Calabria, Italy. He was a Visiting Scholar at the Department of Computer Science and Engineering of the State University of New York at Buffalo. From 2009-2011, he was a Faculty Research Assistant at the University of Maryland Institute for Advanced Computer Studies. Currently, he is an Assistant Professor at the University of Calabria, Italy. His research interests include inconsistency and incompleteness management, logic programming, and social network analysis.

FRANCESCA SPEZZANO

Francesca Spezzano received a Ph.D. in Computer Science Engineering from the University of Calabria, Italy in 2012. She was a Visiting Scholar at the Computer Science Department (Database Group) of the University of California–Santa Cruz from October 2010–July 2011. Currently, she is a Post-Doc Researcher at the University of Calabria, Italy. Her research interests include data exchange, inconsistent databases, and logic programming.